The Parables of Jesus
INVITATIONS TO GRACE

The Parables of Jesus
INVITATIONS TO GRACE

Most Rev. Arthur J. Serratelli
S.T.D., S.S.L., D.D.

CATHOLIC BOOK PUBLISHING CORP.
New Jersey

NIHIL OBSTAT: Rev. T. Kevin Corcoran, MA
Censor Librorum
IMPRIMATUR: ✠ **Most Rev. David M. O'Connell, C.M., J.C.D., D.D.**
Bishop of Trenton
January 10, 2021
The Baptism of the Lord

The Nihil Obstat and Imprimatur are official declarations that a book or pamphlet is free of doctrinal or moral error. No implication is contained therein that those who have granted the Nihil Obstat and Imprimatur agree with the contents, opinions, or statements expressed.

Scripture quotations (unless otherwise noted) are taken from the SAINT JOSEPH NEW CATHOLIC BIBLE ® Copyright © 2019 by Catholic Book Publishing Corp. Used with permission. All rights reserved.

All rights reserved. No part of this book may be reproduced or transmitted in any form or by any means, electronic or mechanical, including photocopying, recording, or by any information storage and retrieval system without permission in writing from the publisher.

(T-934)

ISBN 978-1-953152-08-4

© 2021 by Catholic Book Publishing Corp.
77 West End Rd.
Totowa, NJ 07512
Printed in the U.S.A.

catholicbookpublishing.com

Table of Contents

INTRODUCTION
The Art of Storytelling 6

CHAPTER 1
Jesus the Teacher and His Parables 15

CHAPTER 2
The Parables of the Patch and the New Wine 22

CHAPTER 3
The Parable of the Mustard Seed 34

CHAPTER 4
The Parable of the Wheat and Weeds 48

CHAPTER 5
The Parable of the Two Sons 63

CHAPTER 6
The Parable of the Sheep and Goats 74

CHAPTER 7
The Parable of the Tower of Siloam 91

CHAPTER 8
The Parable of the Barren Fig Tree 99

CHAPTER 9
The Parable of the Narrow Door 113

CHAPTER 10
The Parable of the Prodigal Son 128

CHAPTER 11
The Parable of the Pharisee and the Publican 140

CHAPTER 12
The Parable of the Great Banquet 149

CHAPTER 13
The Parable of the Useless Servant 159

CONCLUSION 167

INTRODUCTION

The Art of Storytelling

From the dawn of civilization, the art of storytelling has been one of the most effective means of communicating values and wisdom from one generation to the next. Our ancient ancestors who lived over 40,000 years ago in caves in Indonesia, Spain, and France began carving on stone the stories they told each other. They wished to leave these stories to those who came after them.

A well-thought-out story does more than simply narrate events. It goes beyond the mere imparting of dry knowledge. It draws the listener or reader into another world. Every story has a truth, a moral, or a new insight wrapped up in its cast of characteristics, setting, and dramatic plot. A good story opens up new ways of understanding. It challenges the listener or reader to think and make judgments.

People of every age have delighted in the tales told to them. In the 6th century B.C., the Greek storyteller Aesop not only entertained but also instructed his audiences with his fables. For three hundred years these stories were repeated by word of mouth before being written down. Yet they never remained imprisoned in a book. Aesop's tale of *The Fox and the Lion* still teaches that "familiarity breeds contempt." His story of *The Hare and the Tortoise* still imparts the wise caution that "slow and steady wins the race." Once stories fall from the lips of the storyteller, they have a life of their own.

In ancient Rome the wealthy would hire professional storytellers to entertain them. They enjoyed having a storyteller accompany them on their long, tedious journeys.

They also employed them for dinners and at other celebrations. In one of his letters, Pliny the Younger, a second century magistrate of Rome, gives an insight into the popularity of storytellers in his day. He tells us that, at local fairs and festivals, storytellers would beckon bystanders to come and listen to them, crying out, "Pay a penny and hear a golden tale." The Roman emperor Augustus even used storytellers to lull him to sleep on restless nights.

For almost two hundred years audiences in Europe enjoyed listening to the stories of King Arthur and his Knights of the Round Table. King Arthur embodied for them the never-ending struggle between good and evil. These tales enthralled and inspired listeners. Then, when Sir Thomas Malory was locked in a London jail in 1460 until his release, he gathered the stories about King Arthur in a book for the first time, thus preserving them for posterity.

No age is without its famous storytellers. The 14th century had the famous English poet Chaucer. In *Canterbury Tales*, he tells the stories of pilgrims on their way from London to the shrine of Saint Thomas Becket at Canterbury Cathedral. The 18th century had Samuel Johnson, the author of one of the most influential dictionaries in the English language. Johnson would meet regularly with other academics for the sheer pleasure of telling stories. As they competed with each other to tell the best story onlookers would listen with delight.

The 19th century had Hans Christian Andersen. Traveling through the Danish countryside, he captured the attention of children with such stories as *The Emperor's New Clothes* and *The Ugly Duckling*. And, the 20th century had Walt Disney. He captivated audiences of all ages. He understood what storytellers do. He once said, "We restore order with imagination. We instill hope again and again and again."

But, of all the storytellers the world has ever known, Jesus is second to none. Jesus is the master storyteller. He steals no one's brush when He paints the vivid images that populate His parables. Both the scholar and the student, the expert and the layperson, can draw inspiration from His parables.

Jesus belonged to a religious and cultural environment that was accustomed to use figurative language to speak of God and His providence. He stands in the tradition of the Hebrew prophets who used images rather than abstract, logical statements to teach and to call others to conversion. The prophet Nathan at the court of King David is a classic example.

It was not unusual for the king to be asked to pass judgment on difficult cases. One day when David was seated on his throne of judgment, Nathan appears before David, feigning to present a case. Unsuspecting, David listens attentively. Nathan tells the parable of "The Poor Man and His Lamb" to uncover David's sins.

> The Lord sent the prophet Nathan to David, and when Nathan arrived, he said to him: "There were two men in a certain town. One was rich and the other was poor. The rich man had flocks and herds in great abundance, but the poor man had nothing at all except for one little ewe lamb which he had bought. He cared for it, and the lamb grew up with him and with his children. It would share the little food he had and drink from his cup and sleep in his arms. It was like a daughter to him.
>
> "On one occasion the rich man welcomed a traveler into his house, but he had no wish to take one

animal from his flock or herd to provide a meal for his guest. Instead he took the poor man's ewe lamb and prepared that for his visitor."

On hearing this, David flew into a rage against that man, and he said to Nathan: "As the Lord lives, the man who has done this deserves to die. He must make fourfold restitution for the lamb, because he has done this without showing the least bit of pity." Then Nathan said to David: "You are that man!"

2 Sam 12:1-7

At the time, Uriah the Hittite, one of David's most trusted soldiers, was away fighting the battle against the Ammonites. David took advantage of his absence and committed adultery with his wife. David was at the height of his reign. Military success after success had crowned him with glory. He was living in a splendid palace, surrounded by luxury. In all the other battles, David had led his army into battle. But this time he sent his general Joab to take his place. He remained behind. David was putting his safety and comfort before the good of his people. His first sin.

It was springtime. The balmy breeze bore the sweet scent of flowers. Rising from his siesta, David took a leisurely stroll on his rooftop terrace. Bathsheba was bathing in her courtyard below. David was captivated by her beauty and desired to have her. Lust, his second sin.

Without the virtue of chastity, there is no self-control. At this point, not even David's harem was enough for him. How can chastity flourish where pleasure reigns? And so David brings Bathsheba to his bed and commits adultery. His third sin.

To conceal his transgression, the unfaithful king arranges for Uriah, the faithful husband of Bathsheba, to be mowed down in battle. Uriah's murder, his fourth sin. From lust to violence is an easy road for the selfish. Indolence, lust, and violence have darkened David's will. And, so like the majestic tree whose roots are rotten, the mighty monarch crashes to the ground from his pinnacle of glory.

David's moral decay happened slowly, but it happened surely. "The moral character of a man is an entire and indivisible thing. It cannot be pure in one part and defiled in another" (Noah Webster, 1801). One sin leads to another. Once on the decline, time and gravity determine how low we go.

David's sins are the greater because he is God's appointed leader of his people. A nation depends on the moral virtue of its leaders. "...When the righteous are in authority, the people rejoice, but they groan when the wicked ascend to power" (Prov 29:2). Written laws are dead letters. But a virtuous leader is a living inspiration for goodness. David's sins of adultery and murder inspired no one.

But God is merciful. He will not suffer His people or His anointed one to languish in sin. He sends the prophet Nathan to call the king to repentance. The king holds in his hands the power over life and death. To accuse any ancient monarch of a crime would have been a dangerous enterprise. This matters little to Nathan. God sends him and he goes. What great courage! Obedience to God always bears good fruit.

The details of the parable which Nathan narrates move David to pity. Sin has not hardened his heart. With just indignation, he instantly passes judgment of guilty on the rich man; and, in so doing, unwittingly condemns himself.

Nathan's words "You are the man!" leave David accused before his entire court. It is a tense moment. Everyone is waiting to hear a word from the king. His response shocks them. No excuse. No attempt to hide his sins. No resentment. At once, he is contrite. He owns his own iniquity. And, for his humble confession of guilt, Nathan assures him of God's forgiveness. No sin is beyond the mercy of God.

Using the art of storytelling, Nathan was able to draw the king into the drama and pathos of the parable of "The Poor Man and His Lamb." The parable captured his emotion and led him to make a just judgment that led to his own conversion. The parable has functioned much more subtly than a sentence of condemnation ever could. For every parable leads the listener to make a response, either positive or negative. By its nature, a parable is transformative, not informative.

Not just Nathan, but other prophets make clever use of the art of storytelling to challenge God's people to amend their ways. Isaiah relates the story of a wasted vineyard (Isa 5:1-7). Jeremiah tells the story of a potter at work making clay vessels (Jer 18:2-6). And, Ezekiel packs his prophecies with story after story, e.g. the lioness and her whelps (Ezr 19:1-9), the eagle and the vine (Ezr 17:2-10), and the dry bones (Ezr 37:1-14).

Not just prophets but others used stories to drive home a truth or bring about a change of attitude or behavior. Thus, Jotham, the youngest of Gideon's sons, recounts his famous fable of the trees choosing a king (Jdg 9: 8-15) to dissuade Israel from becoming a monarchy like other nations. And, a wise woman of Tekoa tells the story of two brothers and revenge (2 Sam 14:5-7) to convince David to forgive his son Absalom for murdering his half-brother Amnon.

Jewish rabbis have always used stories or parables to teach. The Talmud is the central text of rabbinic Judaism. The Jerusalem Talmud was composed in the 4th century A.D.; the Babylonia Talmud in the 5th century A.D. The following example from the Talmud illustrates how the rabbis used the art of storytelling.

> On one occasion Rabbi Eleazar, son of Rabbi Simeon, was coming from Migdal Gedor, from the house of his teacher. He was riding leisurely on his donkey by the riverside and was feeling happy and elated because he had studied much Torah.
>
> There he chanced to meet an exceedingly ugly man who greeted him, "Peace be upon you, rabbi." He, however, did not return his greeting but instead said to him, "Raca (empty one or good for nothing) how ugly you are! Is everyone in your town as ugly as you are?" The man replied, "I do not know, but go and tell the craftsman who made me, 'How ugly is the vessel which you have made.'"
>
> When Rabbi Eleazar realized that he had sinned, he dismounted from the donkey and prostrated himself before the man and said to him, "I submit myself to you, forgive me!"
>
> *Talmud, B. Ta'an. 20a-b1*

In meeting an ugly man, Rabbi Eleazar thinks only about the man's ugliness. Failing to recognize him as someone created in the image and likeness of God, he derides and insults him. His arrogance blinds him to the inherent goodness of the other. But it is otherwise with the less than attractive man.

His sufferings have opened his eyes to the deepest reality of the human person. Everyone comes from the hands of God. Everyone reflects something of the goodness of the Creator and is deserving of respect and love. The not-so-handsome yet humble man knows this better than the self-inflated rabbi.

In this story, the scholar crosses paths with the layman, the learned theologian with the unlettered laborer. The respected scholar rides a donkey; the poor man walks. Yet, in the end who is the wiser? The unattractive man who understands what it means to be created in the image and likeness of God. In the Talmud, this story is offered as a reflection on the biblical account of the creation of humankind.

> God created human beings in his image, in the image of God he created him, male and female He created them. God blessed them and told them, "Be fruitful and multiply, and fill the earth; subdue it and have dominion over the fish of the seas and over the birds of the air and over every living creature that moves upon the earth." *Gen 1:27-28*

This one example typifies how the rabbis were accustomed to use the art of storytelling. They told stories to explain, elucidate, and exemplify a biblical text. They used clever parables to tease out the meaning of Scripture. Their stories are tied to a biblical text and are often capped by a citation from Scripture. In fact, the rabbis extolled the importance of parables by saying: "Let not the parable be lightly esteemed in your eyes, because, by means of a parable, a person can master the words of the Torah" (*Song Rab* 1.1.8).

The rabbis saw the Torah, the first five books of the bible, as a magnificent palace with many rooms. They used their stories as a way to guide the people through all those rooms. Parables made the biblical teaching clear and practical.

The famous theologian Abraham Heschel taught the distinctive value of story over legislative text in Jewish tradition. Law gives knowledge. Stories give inspiration. Law gives us details. Stories give us a vision of living. (Abraham Joshua Heschel, *God in Search of Man: A Philosophy of Judaism*, pp. 336–337).

The rabbinic practice of telling stories spans many centuries. The rabbis told stories about shepherds, kings, farmers, scholars, and feasts. However, nearly all the known parables of the rabbis come from a time after Jesus. Like the rabbis, Jesus used stories as an effective tool in His ministry. But His parables are decidedly different. Jesus used the traditional method of storytelling in a unique way. No surprise. He is the Word Incarnate who speaks the human word as the Son of God!

CHAPTER 1

Jesus the Teacher and His Parables

During His public ministry, the disciples and other individuals addressed Jesus in many different ways. They called Him a prophet, the Messiah, the Lord, and the Son of David. But most often they called Him "Teacher." In the gospels, people call Jesus "Teacher" forty-five times and fourteen times with the similar Aramaic term "Rabbi." Jesus Himself readily accepted the title of teacher. At the Last Supper, He said: "You call me 'Teacher' and 'Lord,' and rightly so, for that is what I am" (Jn 13:13). And with reason!

Jesus, the son of Joseph the carpenter, spent most of His less than three years of public ministry building the kingdom of God by His teaching. This was the noble purpose to which He dedicated himself. Yes, He cast out devils and healed the sick. But He would not let even these good works deter Him from teaching.

Jesus began His ministry in Galilee. "After John had been arrested, Jesus came to Galilee proclaiming the gospel of God" (Mk 1:14). On His first day of public ministry in Capernaum, He fills the day with healing after healing, curing the sick, and driving out demons. The next morning, Peter and the disciples find Him lost in solitary prayer. They try to persuade Him to continue His healing ministry in Capernaum. But Jesus refuses. He says, "Let us move on to the neighboring towns so that I may proclaim the message there as well. For this is the reason why I came" (Mk 1:38).

According to first century Jewish historian Flavius Josephus, Galilee was a densely populated district. There were more than two hundred villages. Each village had several thousand inhabitants. Jesus felt pressed to move beyond His headquarters in Capernaum. He wanted to teach the multitudes in Magdala, Bethsaida, Chorazin, and Gennesaret about the kingdom of God. When Jesus says that He wants to preach in these towns, He is saying much more than what we hear in the word "preach." For us, that word means "to give a sermon" or "to deliver a homily." However, the Greek word κηρύξω (keruso) in Mark 1:38 means "to herald the good news." It means joyfully announcing that the kingdom of God is at hand. Jesus' preaching and teaching were one. In every word Jesus spoke, He sounded the homiletic and didactic. He announced the arrival of the kingdom of God and invited the just and unjust to enter into it (Mk 1:15).

After His first exhausting day of teaching in Capernaum, Jesus withdrew from the crowds and His disciples. He went off to a solitary place for prayer (Mk 1:35). The gospels record four other similar moments in His life. Jesus cures a man of leprosy and then leaves the crowds behind to pray alone (Lk 5:16). Before choosing the Twelve Apostles, He spends the night in prayer on a mountain (Lk 6:12). And, after feeding the five thousand, Jesus dismisses them and goes to pray by Himself (Mt 14:23; Mk 6:46). The disciples are so moved by Jesus' prayer life that they ask Jesus to teach them how to pray (Lk 11:1).

Alone at prayer, Jesus renews His intimacy with the Father. Deep communion with God is always the source of any good work done to others. Those who spend the most time serving others are most in need of their time alone with God. Moses went alone to the top of Mt. Sinai. Elijah to the cave on Mt. Horeb. John the Baptist to the wilderness. Jesus went into the desert and often to lonely places. And so must we. At times, it is best to be apart from those who are closest to us so that we can draw closest to God.

In prayer, Jesus received the power to hold the crowds captive by His teaching so much that they would even go without eating to listen to Him (Mt 15:32). His words enthralled them. From the very first time He teaches in the synagogue of Capernaum, they "were astounded at his teaching, for he taught them as one who had authority, and not as the scribes" (Mk 1:22).

From the time of Ezra the priest in the 6th century B.C., the scribes taught the law to God's people. They explained the Torah by repeating the interpretations of one rabbi after another. Their words had weight inasmuch as they relied on tradition. Not so with Jesus!

Nowhere do we find Jesus citing another rabbi. His teaching is absolute, because His authority is sovereign. His words are "spirit and life" (Jn 6:63). His word alone called forth Lazarus from his tomb. His word can raise us up from our sins now and from the grave on the last day.

Not just the way Jesus spoke with authority but the exciting manner in which He taught held the attention of His listeners. Jesus came from a cultural environment that delighted in using figurative language. Jesus loved to use word pictures, anecdotes, and dramatic stories in teaching about the kingdom of God.

Jesus' teaching and parables are saturated with images of the Galilean countryside. Birds swooping down and eating newly-planted seed. The lilies of the fields clothing the landscape in beauty surpassing Solomon in his finest garments. Wolves among sheep. A reed swayed by the wind. Whitened sepulchers. Jesus was a keen observer of the physical world around Him and He used images from it to impart His spiritual message.

Jesus' parables are found uniquely in the first three gospels. The English word "parable" comes from the Greek παραβολή (parabolē). Among the Greeks, it basically meant an illustration made by comparing one thing to another. But this is too narrow a definition for the parables of Jesus. The Hebrew word for parable (לְמָשָׁל: mashal) includes a wide variety of sayings that use figurative language, whether it be a simile, a metaphor, or a story. These sayings have one thing in common. They are meant to be authoritative and give direction to one's life.

The parables of Jesus may be simply defined as short narratives, taken from the lives of common people and from nature, that capture the attention of the listeners and gently tease them into making a judgment or acknowledging a truth that impacts their lives. With an economy of words, the parables convey a wealth of ideas in a way that can be understood and remembered.

The parables draw their plot from the lives of farmers, shepherds, aristocrats, religious and political leaders, and laborers. Through contrast, exaggeration, humor, and surprise, the parables capture the listener's imagination. A fascinating cast of characters parade through the parables of Jesus. Some are wealthy like the rich man in the parable of Dives and Lazarus (Lk 16:19-31). Others are poor like the woman who loses a single coin (Lk 15:8-10). Some are humorous, such as the widow in the parable of the Unjust Judge (Lk 18:1-8); others, pitiable such as the rich fool (Lk 12:16-21).

Not all the characters in the parables are good, but all are interesting. Some are villains, such as the unmerciful servant (Mt 18:23-35), the wicked tenants (Mt 21:33-46), and the unjust steward who cooks the books (Lk 16:1-8). Others are heroes worthy of imitation, such as the faithful servant (Mk 13:33-37), the Good Samaritan (Lk 10:30-37), and the father of the prodigal son (Lk 15:11-32).

Of all Jesus' teachings, the parables are the most striking. These brief narratives have been enriching the lives of generation after generation. People still speak of being a Good Samaritan, of hiding one's light under a bushel, of paying the last penny.

Jesus' parables make up well over a third of His teaching. They are thoroughly original. In telling these stories, Jesus is the master storyteller, able to ignite the imagination of a child as well as tease the mind of the scholar. Listening to the parables puts us in touch with the words of Jesus as He spoke them during His public ministry.

In His parables, Jesus serves up His wisdom with a healthy seasoning of humor. He pokes fun at the rich man, hoarding His goods in bigger and bigger barns, only to die and leave them to someone else to enjoy (Lk 12:16-20). He mocks the unjust judge, because He literally fears being punched under the eye by a poor, nagging widow (Lk 18:1-5). Jesus makes many serious points in humorous ways. In this way, like a wise surgeon, Jesus exposes the ills of humanity not to embarrass but to heal.

We are so accustomed to hear the parables in the somber setting of church that we can easily miss their humor. Furthermore, our culture and our sense of humor differ from those of Jesus' first century audience. Nonetheless, with even a little attention, we can appreciate and even enjoy the humor in the parables.

For example, when some Pharisees criticize Jesus for not observing all their human laws of ritual purity, He denounces them as "blind guides, you strain out a gnat and then swallow a camel" (Mt 23:24). We can readily understand this barbed hyperbole. How could someone who is blind even see a tiny gnat to strain it out? How could anyone swallow a camel?

This terse and ludicrous comparison of the Pharisees to blind guides would have evoked laughter. But there is more. In His native Aramaic, Jesus is making a pun. The word for gnat is *galma*. The word for camel is *gamla*. The play on words in Jesus' spoken language would have delighted the ears of His listeners, but it is lost on ours.

Jesus was a master at injecting humor in His parables, sometimes by wordplays, or irony or satire, but most often by exaggeration. When Jesus wants to speak about the gravity of our sins and our utter incapacity to reconcile ourselves with God, He talks about a king whose servant owed him ten thousand talents (Mt 18:23-35). The amount of this debt would have shocked Jesus' audience and the king's response would have surprised them even more.

In Jesus' day, workers earned only one talent every twenty years. The stated amount of ten thousand talents, that is, four and half billion dollars, would have left them scratching their heads! How could the king forgive such a debt? They would have just stood there looking at one another in amazement.

With His sense of humor, Jesus could sketch a memorable picture in just a word or two. For example, in a moment of innocent play, Jesus names James and John "sons of thunder" (Mk 3:17). They earned this epithet because they wanted Jesus to call down fire to destroy the Samaritans for not welcoming Jesus (Lk 9:53-54).

Likewise, in preaching the Sermon on the Mount, Jesus uses humor to get His message across. To counsel His disciples to preach the gospel effectively without uselessly squandering their efforts, Jesus coins the lighthearted proverb "...do not cast your pearls before swine" (Mt 7:6). With this comical image of pigs mistaking pearls for grain, He captures the response of those whose sin has dulled their ability to recognize the truth of the gospel.

With His parables, Jesus touches on serious issues. Hypocrisy. Greed. Mercy. Forgiveness. Repentance. Obedience to God's will. Justice. And Love. He addressed His teaching not just to the eager, but to the hostile. What better way to reach both than through humor! Humor disarms hostility. It breaks down barriers. It puts people at ease and makes them more willing to listen to Jesus. Jesus preferred light-hearted humor to somber rigidity in ushering in the kingdom of God.

Jesus uses humor because He Himself is a man of immense joy. The Father had anointed Him with the oil of gladness beyond all His companions (Ps 45:8). He speaks the parables to open our hearts to that same joy. As Jesus says at the Last Supper, "These things I have spoken to you, that my joy may be in you, and that your joy may be full" (Jn 15:11).

Jesus' dour adversaries recoiled at the way Jesus behaved. He was too joyful for them (Lk 7:33-35). But He could not be otherwise. Through His preaching, God was sweeping away all sins. He was beginning even in this world the great feast "where people will come from the east and the west and from the north and the south and will recline at table in the kingdom of God" (Lk 13:29). With His parables, Jesus is opening our ears to hear God say, "Come and share your master's joy" (Mt 25:21,23).

CHAPTER 2

The Parables of the Patch and the New Wine

Marcion was one of the most important figures in second century Christianity. He was a wealthy ship owner and merchant from Sinope, located on the Turkish side of the Black Sea. Sometime in the late 130s A.D., Marcion went to Rome and began teaching his ideas about the faith. Most notably, he taught that the god of the Old Testament was a god of wrath and the god of the New Testament was the god of love.

Marcion held that the capricious god of Judaism was a lesser deity who created the material world with all that is evil and oppressive. This god was distinct from the compassionate, loving, merciful, and forgiving god of the New Testament. So aberrant were his teachings that he held the distinction of being the heretic most often attacked by the Greek and Latin theologians of his day.

Marcion's basic error was his adamant refusal to accept that the God of the Old Testament was indeed the Father whom Jesus preached. He thus placed a radical discontinuity between the teaching of the Old Testament and that of the New Testament. This led him to discard the Old Testament and produce his own bible, selectively editing out those passages of Luke and Paul that did not fit his teaching.

It took almost two centuries before his teachings died out. Nonetheless, his false ideas survive in those who say that Jesus came to displace Judaism. Some read the following two short parables as if Jesus Himself was giving His blessing to this displacement of the Old Testament teaching by His own teaching.

The Parables of the Patch and New Wine

> No one sews a piece of unshrunken cloth on an old cloak. If he does, the patch pulls away, the new from the old, and a worse tear results.
>
> Nor does anyone pour new wine into old wineskins. If he does, the wine will burst the skins, and then the wine and the skins are both lost. Rather, new wine is poured into fresh wineskins.   *Mk 2:21-22*

Many interpret these sayings of Jesus as a strong rejection of Jewish practices. They say that Jesus comes to replace the old, worn-out garment of Jewish belief with the new wine of Christianity. They say that He is arguing against trying to accommodate what He teaches about the freedom of the Spirit with the rituals of the past. Such an understanding of Jesus' teaching is superficial and misguided.

All three evangelists record the twin parables of the Patch and the parable of the New Wine (Mk 2:21-22; Mt 9:16-17; Lk 5:36-39). In each gospel, the context is the same. Jesus calls Levi, the tax-collector, to follow Him. Levi accepts the call and gives a banquet to celebrate with his friends. The disciples of the Pharisees and some followers of John the Baptist complain. They are upset because Jesus and His disciples do not fast as they do. Jesus responds to their dismay with the twin parables. First, let us examine the parables; and, then, the context.

The parable of not repairing a rent in an old garment with a patch of new cloth is common sense. To take a piece of cloth that had not been prepared, that is, pre-shrunk, and to sew it onto an old garment, would cause a tear. Such a clumsy procedure would ruin the garment. Thus, Jesus sees His mission not as patching up the old. His preaching is not simply to make up for the inadequacies of what went before. His ministry of mercy and forgiveness is something much more.

He repeats the same idea with the parable of the New Wine. Wineskins were made of animal skin, usually from a goat. When new the wineskin is soft and flexible. When used and old it dries out and becomes stiff. Pouring new wine into old wineskins would be foolish.

New wine continues to ferment. A worn-out wineskin would not be flexible enough to expand with the fermenting wine. It would simply burst, spilling the wine and destroying the container. Thus, new wine must be poured into containers made of fresh wineskins. These would be supple enough to allow the new wine to breathe and expand. They would be strong enough to absorb the bubbling energy of the fermenting wine and not split open.

With this second parable, Jesus is completing the parable of the Patch. He is not saying that the Jewish dispensation is so worn out and decayed, so inflexible, that it is being replaced by His ministry. Some interpret it this way. But this does not fit the context. Jesus is reinforcing the idea that something new and intoxicating is happening in His ministry. But He is not disparaging the old.

From the very beginning, Jesus' ministry strikes an unexpected note of compassion and openness to all. He welcomes sinners. He offers forgiveness and mercy in a way unlike the Pharisees and even unlike John the Baptist. For example, Jesus invites Himself to the house of the hated tax-collector Zacchaeus. Joy-filled at Jesus' acceptance of him, Zacchaeus, small in stature, becomes big in heart, generously giving away his ill-gotten wealth in reparation for his sins. Jesus' words of grace lead him to repentance and to joy.

For those who accept Him, Jesus is the Savior whose very coming on earth is news of great joy to all the people (Lk 2:10). Jesus offers a path to God not without sacrifice but always with joy. Following Jesus does not restrict one's horizons but opens one to embrace life in its fullness.

A careful look at the context where Jesus tells the twin parables of the Patch and the New Wine shows that Jesus does not discard what came before Him. Rather, He brings all that God revealed in the Old Testament to completion. As Jesus Himself said, "Do not think that I have come to abolish the Law or the Prophets. I have come not to abolish but to fulfill them" (Mt 5:17). For just as the sun rises in the sky, giving more and more light, so too God slowly enlightens the world through the gradual revelation of His Word, beginning in the Old Testament and culminating with the New Testament.

The context of the twin parables of the Patch and the New Wine is the beginning of Jesus' public ministry. Jesus has begun to call certain individuals to be His disciples. Walking along the Sea of Galilee, He saw Simon (Peter) and Andrew, James and John in the midst of working as fishermen (Mk 1:16-20). He called them and they left everything to follow Him.

These men were hard workers, often working long into the night. Fishing taught them how to deal with efforts that do not produce immediate results. They knew how to be patient and not become discouraged. They were well prepared for their future work as apostles. For us as well, patience and determination are essential to follow Jesus faithfully. Patience is not simply waiting but waiting with an attitude of hope. "Whoever is out of patience is out of possession of their soul" (Francis Bacon).

Some days after calling the first four disciples, Jesus teaches the crowds by the sea (Mk 2:13). When He is finished, He passes by the tax collector's booth near the Sea of Galilee. He sees Levi (Matthew) sitting there, collecting road tolls, harbor dues, and taxes on goods from those passing through the territory of Herod Antipas. Jesus calls Levi.

"Levi left everything, and got up and followed him" (Lk 5:28). The word "followed" (ἠκολούθει: ēkolouthei) is in the imperfect tense. It means that Levi at that moment begins to follow Jesus and then continues to follow Him. Discipleship is a lifelong journey with the Lord. Each day we need to renew our decision to be Jesus' disciples.

Overjoyed by Jesus' call, Levi scurries off and gathers all his friends for a feast. Both Mark and Matthew tell us that Jesus reclines at table in Levi's house. Luke gives us more details. He tells us that this is no small dinner for a select few. Levi, a wealthy man, is extravagant in showing his joy. He invites a large crowd of his friends and acquaintances for a great feast (Lk 5:29). And not just any feast. It is a feast with a purpose. Luke uses the word "banquet" (δοχή: dochē) that comes from the Greek word meaning "to receive someone as a guest." The banquet in Levi's house is a reception given in honor of Jesus, the new rabbi.

At this reception, there pulsates through Levi's heart an exhilarating feeling, a moral elevation. Others hold him in contempt because of his work. He is a living reminder of the Roman occupation. They shun him. But not Jesus! In gratitude, Levi invites his fellow tax collectors and other outcasts to dine with him and Jesus. He wants them to hear Jesus. Gratitude for God's blessing always overflows into charity to others. Kindness truly received becomes kindness generously shared. It always brings joy.

Jesus is quite comfortable in Levi's house. Throughout His ministry, Jesus is often found at table with others. He

The Parables of the Patch and New Wine

uses the meal as a means of introducing a new standard of social values. Sitting at table with the outcasts and the marginalized, Jesus overturns the exclusiveness of the religious and social elite. Every person, even those shunned by society, are loved by God and called to the banquet of life. Jesus' meals with others are a foretaste of the feast to be shared in the kingdom of God. His eating with the marginalized challenges us not to exclude others from our love.

While Jesus is enjoying the sumptuous reception Levi sets before Him and savoring his choice wine, some Pharisees and disciples of John the Baptist become disturbed by His behavior. They object. How is it that they fast, but Jesus' disciples do not? (Mk 2:18). Jesus' critics shrink from directly assailing Him. They take His followers to task. They ask about His disciples' not fasting at the very moment when Jesus is feasting. They are really attacking the Master Himself.

Although the law only mandated fasting on Yom Kippur, the Day of Atonement, pious Jews observed many other days of fasting (Isa 58:3). In Jesus' day, the Pharisees fasted every Thursday and Monday. According to tradition, on these days, Moses had ascended and descended Mt. Sinai.

John the Baptist was a stern ascetic. He himself fasted (Lk 7:33). No doubt his disciples followed his example. John had pointed out Jesus as the Messiah to his followers. But, when they saw Jesus in the midst of merriment, associating with sinners, they were shocked. How can Jesus be the Messiah for whom they had been preparing to welcome by their fasting and penance? His very manner of life was making them unsure of the way they had chosen to please God.

Some of their own company, like Andrew, had joined the crowds following Jesus. They were no longer fasting as they had been when they were disciples of John the Baptist. Those who remained with John may have been jealous at what seemed to be the easier spirituality of their former companions. Jealousy is always a symptom of insecurity. To those questioning Jesus why His disciples do not fast, Jesus says,

> How can the wedding guests [literally, "the sons of the bridal chamber"] fast while the bridegroom is still with them? As long as they have the bridegroom with them, they cannot fast. But the time will come when the bridegroom is taken away from them, and then on that day they will fast.   *Mk 2:19-20*

What a beautiful way Jesus images His own ministry! Jesus is calling His followers to be part of the greatest event of time. Jesus is issuing the invitation to come to the banquet of heaven which "the Lord of hosts will provide for all peoples, a feast of rich food and choice wines, juicy, rich food and pure, choice wines" (Isa 25:6). Jesus is the happy bridegroom beginning His marriage feast. And Jesus' disciples share His joy. No sadness, no fasting, no tears!

Jesus uses the familiar customs of a wedding celebration to silence those who are criticizing Him. According to the Jewish tradition, "the sons of the bridal chamber" (the friends of the groom) would bring the bride to the home of her husband for the wedding. Then they would feast and celebrate for seven days.

So essential was the ritual of rejoicing at the wedding feast that the Talmud absolved the friends of the bridegroom from prayer and worship. Just as wedding guests do not fast and mourn while the marriage celebration is

The Parables of the Patch and New Wine

taking place, so too Jesus' disciples do not fast, because they are with Jesus, who is the bridegroom.

With His answer, Jesus is reminding the disciples of John the Baptist of what their own teacher himself had said to them about Jesus. They had come to John upset that Jesus was beginning to baptize just as John was doing (Jn 3:22). They saw this as a threat to John's ministry. But John did not! John told his disciples:

> You yourselves can testify that I said [that] I am not the Christ. I have been sent before him. It is the bridegroom who has the bride, but the friend of the brideroom who stands by and listens for him rejoices greatly when he hears the bridegroom's voice. This joy of mine is complete. *Jn 3:28-29*

The Baptist had taught his followers that Jesus was the bridegroom whose coming filled John with joy. The time of waiting was now over.

John understood himself as the one pointing to Jesus. Jesus was the greater. He tells his followers, "He must increase, but I must decrease" (Jn 3:30). Because he was humble, he was content with his role as precursor and rejoiced in Jesus' mission. "There is something in humility which strangely exalts the heart" (Saint Augustine).

In referring to Himself as the bridegroom, Jesus is not merely contrasting His ministry of joy and feasting with John's ministry of penance and fasting. He is doing more than saying that John prepared for His arrival. He is giving the profound reason why there is joy in His presence.

The Old Testament prophets use marriage to explain the relationship of God with His people. With the image of the marriage bond, they refer to God as the husband or bridegroom. The nation He chose for Himself is His bride or the wife. The prophet Hosea sees his own passionate love for Gomer, his unfaithful wife, as a way to understand God's love for unfaithful Israel (Hos 1-3).

Other prophets as well make use of this same imagery. Isaiah, the 8th century prophet whom Jesus cites more than any other prophet, says,

> For your Creator has now become your husband;
> his name is the Lord of hosts.
> The Holy One of Israel is your redeemer;
> he is called the God of the entire world. *Isa 54:5*

Likewise, in chastising Israel for her infidelity to the covenant, Jeremiah says,

> Go forth and proclaim this message in the hearing of Jerusalem:
> I remember the devotion you displayed in your youth,
> your love like that of a bride,
> when you followed me through the desert,
> through a land that was unsown. *Jer 2:2*

In light of these Old Testament prophecies, Jesus' appropriation of the image of bridegroom and bride to describe His relationship to His disciples is astonishing. He is placing himself in the role reserved for God himself. This indicates Christ's self-consciousness. He knows that He is God who has come to unite humanity with God. In His coming among us, the wedding feast has begun. It is a time for joy, not fasting.

With fasting itself, Jesus has no problem. During the temptations in the desert, He himself fasted (Mt 4:1-11; Mk 1:12-13; Lk 4:1-4). In the Sermon on the Mount, He counseled His followers:

> Whenever you fast, do not assume a gloomy expression like the hypocrites who contort their faces so that others may realize that they are fast-

The Parables of the Patch and New Wine

ing. Amen, I say to you, they have received their reward. But when you fast, put oil on your head and wash your face, so that the fact that you are fasting will not be obvious to others but only to your Father who is hidden. And your Father who sees everything that is done in secret will reward you.   *Mt 6:16-18*

Jesus tells those questioning Him that His own disciples one day will fast. "The time will come when the bridegroom is taken away (ἀπαρθῇ) from them, and then on that day they will fast" (Mk 2:20). But not now! They will fast when he "is taken away from them."

All three synoptic gospels use the same Greek word ἀπαρθῇ (aparthē) to speak of Jesus' "being taken away" from His disciples. It is a word that occurs only here in the entire New Testament. It means "to take away, lift off or snatch away." It conveys the idea of a painful end or severance.

The use of this word is significant. It shows that the thought of His own death is with Jesus even as He begins His public ministry. In the midst of a festive social gathering, in the criticism of those who oppose His mission, Jesus sees a dim foreshadowing of the Cross when He will be violently taken from His disciples. In Mark's gospel, this is the first recorded allusion to Jesus' death.

After Jesus leaves His disciples, then will be the proper time for fasting and penance. But not now. Jesus is in their midst. Jesus' presence among His disciples fulfills the prophecy of the 7th century prophet Zephaniah.

After announcing judgment on the southern kingdom of Judah, the prophet promised great mercy. Zephaniah looked to the time of the Messiah when God was going to take away the sins of His people and fill them with joy by His very presence in their midst. He says,

> Cry out with joy, daughter of Zion;
> shout aloud, O Israel.
> Rejoice and exult with all your heart,
> O daughter, Jerusalem.
> The Lord has canceled the punishments against you;
> he has turned away your enemies.
> The king of Israel, the Lord, is in your midst;
> you need never again fear any harm....
> The Lord, your God, is in your midst,
> a warrior and a savior.
> He will rejoice over you with gladness
> and renew you through his love.
> He will exult over you with shouts of joy...
>
> *Zep 3:14-15,17*

Zephaniah's exuberant words overflow with joy because God is in the midst of His people as their savior. Daughter Zion is called to rejoice in God because God rejoices in her. What a magnificent image! We are to be joyful because God is in our midst, rejoicing over us. We are to exult with gladness because God Himself sings for joy over us.

What the prophet once said has come to fulfillment in the coming of Christ among us. This intimate fellowship, this communion between God and us, gives birth to God's joy in us and our joy in God. What makes us holy makes us happy.

In conclusion, we can now better understand Jesus' twin parables of an old patch on a new garment and new wine in new wineskins. His purpose is not to distance Himself from His Jewish roots, as if they were to be dug up and cast aside with something totally new planted in their place. Rather, Jesus uses these two parables to emphasize the unbounded joy that accompanies the coming of the kingdom through His ministry of mercy and forgiveness.

Jesus brings the new wine. There is a new impetus, a new energy, a freshness to His teaching. The Old Testament prepared for this moment and now is coming to fulfillment. The practices of the past are not swept away. They are given new meaning because the intimate communion, the abiding of God with His people, is consummated in Jesus. The new wineskins are those who receive Jesus and are willing to expand their circle of love to embrace all. There is no need to patch an old garment with cloth from a new one. God Himself is providing the wedding garment for the feast that has already begun.

CHAPTER 3

The Parable of the Mustard Seed

During the period of the Cold War (1947-1991), the United States and Russia came very close to a full-scale nuclear war. On July 26, 1963, President Kennedy delivered his historic *Limited Nuclear Test Ban Treaty Address to the Nation*. He saw the agreement between the United States and the Soviet Union as the beginning of something desperately needed. At the end of his speech, he quoted the 6th century B.C. Chinese philosopher Laozi, a contemporary of Confucius, who said, "A journey of a thousand miles must begin with a single step." Here is a truth repeated often by philosophers, teachers, writers, and motivational speakers: great initiatives arise from small beginnings.

In commenting on the life of Demosthenes, the greatest of Ancient Greece's orators, the historian Plutarch wrote, "Small opportunities are often the beginning of great and mighty enterprises." Similarly, John Dryden, 17th century English poet and playwright, once quipped, "Mighty things from small beginnings grow." No surprise that Jesus, the greatest teacher who ever graced the face of the earth, would use the mustard seed, so small and seemingly insignificant, to reveal the great mystery of the kingdom of God.

After hearing Jesus tell the parable of the Sower and the Seed to the crowds (Mk 4:1-9, 13-20; Mt 13:1-9, 18-23), the disciples become despondent. The parable speaks not simply about the success of the Word of God preached in their ministry, but unapologetically about the failure that awaits them. The seed which falls on the

The Parable of the Mustard Seed

pathway, on rocky ground and among the thorns comes to naught. Only the seed sown on good soil takes root and flourishes. In effect, seventy-five percent of the sower's effort is lost. Only twenty-five percent produces success.

The disciples understand what Jesus is saying. Most of their preaching will not yield great results. However, Jesus spoke many parables to help them understand the mystery of the kingdom of God (Mk 4:33). No single parable teaches all there is to say about it. And, so to encourage His disheartened disciples, Jesus tells them the parable of the Mustard Seed.

He said, "With what shall we compare the kingdom of God, or what parable can we use to explain it? It is like a mustard seed that, when it is sown in the ground, is the smallest of all the seeds on the earth. But once it is sown, it springs up and becomes the greatest of all plants, and it puts forth large branches so that the birds of the air can make nests in its shade."   *Mk 4:30-32*

The black mustard seed was well-known in Jesus' day. It was amazingly small. One-sixty-fourth of an inch. In popular language, the smallest of all the seeds. Among the rabbis, the size of the seed grown to full stature was proverbial. "Rabbi Joseph related: 'It once happened to a man at Shinin to whom his father had left three twigs of mustard that one of them split and was found to contain nine kab of mustard, and its timber sufficed to cover a potter's hut.'" (*B.Ket.*111b)

But comparing the kingdom of God to a mustard seed would have struck Jesus' disciples as strange. Jesus' audience would have expected Him to use the mighty oak or noble cedar to image the kingdom of God. These trees of great strength and size would better symbolize for them the kingdom that they were awaiting. The vision of the prophet Daniel had conditioned them to think of the kingdom of God as a vast dominion.

> As the night visions continued,
>   I beheld approaching on the clouds of heaven
>   one like a son of man.
> He came before the Ancient One
>   and was presented to him.
> Dominion and glory and kingship
>   were conferred upon him
> so that all peoples and nations of every language
>   would become his servants.
> His dominion is an everlasting dominion
>   that will never pass away,
> and his kingdom is one
>   that will never be destroyed. *Dan 7:13-14*

Jesus' use of the mustard seed further shocks His disciples. They were not unfamiliar with rabbis using the illustration of the mustard seed. But the rabbis never did so in a religious teaching. The vine. The olive tree. The fig tree. These they used. But never the mustard plant. It was too common a plant to bear the freight of their religious instruction.

Traveling along the roads and walking through the fields, Jesus often noticed the mustard plant. It grew, blossomed, produced its seed and then died at the end of the season. So ordinary! But not for Jesus. For Him, all nature spoke of the greatness of God. Jesus saw in this common garden herb something of the mystery of the kingdom of God. As St. Paul reminds us, "Ever since the creation of the world the invisible attributes of god's eternal power and divine nature have been clearly understood and perceived through the things he has made" (Rom 1:20). All creation bears the signature of the Creator.

The Parable of the Mustard Seed

Jesus points to the insignificant mustard seed sown in the soil and then immediately says, "It springs up and becomes the largest of plants and puts forth large branches, so that the birds of the sky can dwell in its shade." From the small seed comes a shrub as tall as an eight-foot or ten-foot tree. It was so large that it would take three men holding hands to get their arms around its trunk! Perhaps this is why Matthew and Luke call it a tree. It looks like one.

In the parable, Jesus ignores the type of soil and the sower sowing the seed. Only the size of the full grown plant interests Him. The tiny seed one moment, the great shrub the next. In effect, Jesus is telling His disciples not to lose hope. Although the effects of His ministry seem so negligible, nonetheless, His ministry is actually ushering a vast new reality.

The parable of the Mustard Seed gives us hope. Jesus is bringing about a kingdom that extends its borders beyond Israel. The world so often stands against teachings of Jesus and His Church. Yet the Church continues to grow. Cut down, she rises again, converting opposition into opportunity and enemies into friends. Each day, the Church is becoming a home, a place of refuge, for all people of every race and nation, language and culture. All by the power of God working within her.

By mentioning the birds resting in the large branches of the fully grown mustard tree, Jesus evokes a biblical image. When Daniel interprets King Nebuchadnezzar's cryptic dream, he tells him that the tree with the birds in its branches symbolizes his vast and powerful kingdom.

> The tree that you saw, which grew great and strong, with its top touching the sky so that it could be seen throughout the entire earth, a tree with beau-

tiful foliage and abundant fruit, providing food for all and affording shade for the wild beasts, with the birds of heaven dwelling in its branches—that tree is you, O king. You have grown great and strong! Your power has increased and now reaches the sky, your sovereignty extends to the ends of the earth.

Dan 4:17-19

At the end of the Babylonian Exile, the prophet Ezekiel stirs up the hope of a broken people by announcing that God Himself is about to restore His people to their land. He will establish Israel as a new kingdom.

Thus says the Lord:
I myself will break off a tender shoot
 from the highest branch of a tall cedar
 and plant it on a high and lofty mountain.
On the highest mountain in Israel I will plant it
 so that it may put forth branches and bear fruit
 and become a majestic cedar.
Birds of every kind will live beneath it;
 in the shelter of its branches
 winged creatures of every kind will dwell.

Ezek 17:22-23

In Ezekiel, the image of the birds of the heavens taking shelter in a tree emphasizes the great expanse of the kingdom of Israel. In Daniel, it symbolizes the vast extension of Nebuchadnezzar's kingdom. And, in the parable of the mustard seed, it foretells the wide embrace of the kingdom of God. But, in the parable, the image says this and something more.

The large mustard shrub extends its arms to welcome all birds of the sky. The birds do not merely come to perch on its branches and rest in its shade. They come to stay. The Greek word in the text κατασκηνοῦν (kataskēnoun) means "to encamp" or "to dwell." Thus, the birds from every quarter of the heavens come not merely to find shelter from sun, but to build their nests and make their home there. What an apt symbol for the kingdom of God that welcomes all! A home for all peoples of the world!

Interesting enough, the Greek word used for the birds dwelling in the tree's branches is the very same word used for God making His dwelling among His people (Ex 25:8, 29:4; Jn 1:14). Thus, in a typological sense, the mustard tree symbolizes the Church, where God dwells among His people. By our faith in Jesus, we are made "into a holy temple in the Lord; in him [we] also are being built together into a dwelling place for God in the Spirit" (Eph 2:21-22).

The word "to dwell" means "to stay, to remain, to abide, to put down stakes, to set up a home." Where we dwell, we make a permanent home. Our dwelling is where we live life, carrying out our daily duties and growing in love. And there God is. "Do you not know that you are the temple of God?" (1 Cor 3:16).

Furthermore, when we praise God in good times and bad, He is most pleased. For, as the psalmist says, "God inhabits the praises of his people" (Ps 22:3). God is never far from us at prayer. His presence makes every home a sanctuary and every work a means to build up the kingdom of God.

Hidden within the parable of the Mustard Seed is the story of Jesus Himself. For centuries, the Jews waited for the Messiah. They nourished the hope of His coming to make them a great nation again. They eagerly stretched their eyes, looking for the Messiah with great longing. Some had mistakenly identified Cyrus the Persian as the Messiah; others, Alexander the Great. A powerful figure.

A strong ruler. A Messiah to free them from oppression and restore them to their former glory. That was their hope.

But Jesus did not match the Messianic expectations of His people. He came from Galilee, an obscure corner of the Roman Empire. He worked as a carpenter in Nazareth, a town not even mentioned in the Old Testament. When Jesus emerged in His thirtieth year from the confines of His family and hometown, He became an itinerant rabbi. For a few years, He taught in towns and villages, occasionally going to Jerusalem. He gathered only a few loyal followers; and, they came mostly from the poor and uneducated. This was not the profile of the expected Messiah.

Jesus knew the hearts of His disciples. He knew that they were getting discouraged. Even as they began to recognize Him as the Messiah, they were becoming disappointed that He was not going to take up arms and wage a battle against Rome. Soon they would be totally disheartened by His death. And so Jesus offers them the mustard seed as a way of understanding God's plan for our salvation. In His words of mercy and deeds of grace, the kingdom of God is already present just as the great mustard tree is present in the tiny mustard seed. In Jesus, the kingdom of God! On two other occasions, Jesus made this same point that where He is, there is the kingdom of God.

Once a demoniac who was blind and mute was brought to Jesus. When the crowds saw Jesus heal the man, they began to ask, "Is this not the Son of David?" (Mt 12:23). Alarmed at the Messianic excitement of the people, the Pharisees immediately accuse Jesus of being in league with the devil. Even the noblest of our deeds are subject at times to the calumny of those whose hearts are not right with God.

Jesus hears the Pharisees whispering against Him. With devastating logic, Jesus dismantles their argument. Satan cannot be self-destructive. "If Satan drives out Satan, he is divided against himself; how then can his kingdom survive?" (Mt 12:26). Only harmony and cooperation bring stability to a kingdom. Evil is always self-destructive. Whether in the spiritual or in the political domain, where citizens war against each other for power, the nation itself collapses.

Jesus completely foils their accusation by asking, "If it is by Beelzebul that I cast out demons, by whom do your own children cast them out? Therefore, they will be your judges?" (Mt 12:27). Then, after defeating the malicious attack of His adversaries, Jesus announces, "If it is by the Spirit of God that I cast out demons, then the kingdom of God has come to you" (Mt 12:28). Jesus is ushering in the kingdom. It is not some far off reality. The kingdom is present in Jesus.

On another occasion, the Pharisees taunted Jesus. He had been preaching that the kingdom of God was at hand. But they saw in His ministry none of the signs that they expected. No power. No splendor. No royal dignity. They bluntly asked Jesus when the kingdom of God was coming. He responded, "The coming of the kingdom of God will not occur with signs that can be observed. Nor will people say, 'Here it is,' or, 'There it is.' For the kingdom of God is among you" (Lk 17:20-21).

In the sentence "the kingdom of God is among you," the Greek phrase for "among you" (ἐντὸς ὑμῶν: entos humon) is sometimes translated "within you." This translation has Jesus telling the Pharisees that the kingdom of God is not the visible kingdom of power that they were expecting. Rather, it is a spiritual reality already at work in their hearts. But this does not fit the context. It is hardly possible that Jesus would be telling those who reject Him that the kingdom of God is already in them.

The Greek soldier Xenephon translates the same Greek phrase ἐντὸς ὑμῶν (entos humon) as "in the midst of your ranks" (*Anabasis* i. 10, 3). This translation makes better sense in Jesus' situation. Facing His adversaries, Jesus is courageously telling them that, in Him who stands in their midst, the kingdom is present. The kingdom is present in Him as the plant is already present in the seed.

During Jesus' last Passover, all Jerusalem was buzzing with the news of Jesus' Palm Sunday entrance as Messiah. A group of Greeks who came to worship in Jerusalem wanted to see Jesus. They go to Philip. A natural choice. Philip comes from Bethsaida. He had contact with the Greeks of the Decapolis. He most likely spoke their language. They asked him, "Sir, we would like to see Jesus" (Jn 12:21). Philip understands their request. The day John the Baptist had pointed out Jesus as the Messiah, Philip became so excited that he ran to Nathaniel and he himself invited him, saying, "Come and see [Jesus]" (Jn 1:46). Now the Greeks want to see Jesus.

Philip hands over to Andrew, his close collaborator, the task of introducing the inquisitive Greeks to Jesus. A logical choice. Andrew had brought his own brother Peter to Jesus (Jn 1:41). And, in the miracle of the multiplication of the loaves and fish, he brought the boy with five barley loaves and two fish to Jesus (Jn 6:8-9). What a great model to follow! Every good Christian looks for ways to bring others to Jesus.

When Andrew informs Jesus that the Greeks are eager to see Him, Jesus begins to speak of His imminent death.

The Parable of the Mustard Seed 43

To the Greeks just as for the Jews, it was very strange that the Messiah must die to achieve His mission. And so Jesus explains the purpose of His death in a way both could understand. For the Jews, He draws His lesson from the Torah. For the Greeks, from nature.

Early in Jesus' public ministry, Nicodemus had come to Jesus to question Him. He was a respected member of the Sanhedrin. He came at night not to compromise his standing in the eyes of the other members of the Jewish high court. If his visit were to become known, he would incur the hostility of other Pharisees.

Nicodemus was a professionally trained teacher. Nonetheless, he addresses Jesus, the Galilean carpenter, with great respect. "Rabbi, we know that you are a teacher who has come from God" (Jn 3:2). Nicodemus may not be so courageous, coming secretly; but, he is honest and sincere. Sincerity is the condition of true friendship. And Nicodemus is beginning a lasting friendship with Jesus.

At the end of Jesus' life, Nicodemus appears again. At Jesus' trial, he demands that the Sanhedrin allow Jesus to defend Himself (Jn 7:50-51). Then, after the crucifixion, he joins with Joseph of Arimathea in giving Jesus a decent burial (Jn 19:39-42). The amount of balm they used in anointing Jesus for burial was quite extraordinary. No ordinary burial. It was the burial of a king.

At the beginning of Jesus' ministry, Nicodemus had sought the truth. By the end of Jesus' life, he found it by becoming a believer in Jesus. No longer a hesitant inquirer but a courageous believer. As with Nicodemus and Jesus, every true friendship is a story of transformation to the better.

In explaining the salvific meaning of His future death, Jesus uses a biblical image familiar to Nicodemus. During the Exodus the Israelites became weary of their journey to the Promised Land. They rebelled against God. As a punishment, God sent a plague. Poisonous serpents bit the people in the wilderness causing burning pain and death.

When the Israelites repented and cried out for mercy, God instructed Moses to make a brass serpent and to put it on a pole. All who looked up at the serpent were healed. This was not magic. The serpent of brass lifted up by Moses represented God's will to heal the people. Those who looked on it, believing in the power and mercy of God, were healed. It was their faith in God's word that brought spiritual forgiveness and bodily healing (Num 21:4-9).

In Nicodemus' nocturnal visit, Jesus refers back to this event of the Exodus to enlighten him on the mystery of Jesus' own death as Messiah. "Just as Moses lifted up the serpent in the desert, so must the Son of Man be lifted up, so that everyone who believes in him may have eternal life" (Jn 3:14-15). Jesus lifted up on the Cross is not a mere symbol of God's will to save. The Crucified Jesus is the eternal love of God made manifest. Those who look at the Cross with faith, believing in God's plan of salvation, have their sins forgiven. By His death, Christ destroys the venom of sin and the sting of death. The Messiah's death is not a mere accident. It belongs to God's eternal plan of salvation.

When the Greeks come to Him during the last days of His life, Jesus explains His death as Messiah, not with a teaching from Scripture, but with an image they readily understand. Greek curiosity for nature was well known. And so Jesus turns to nature. He says, "Amen, amen, I say to you, unless a grain of wheat falls to the ground and dies, it remains just a grain of wheat; but if it dies, it produces much fruit" (Jn 12:24). The grain of wheat seeded in the

The Parable of the Mustard Seed

ground must die for its life to burst forth into something greater. The kingdom is present in Jesus while He is on earth, but when He dies, it will burst forth in its fullness.

Although this encounter of the Greeks with Jesus seems almost casual and insignificant, it is the beginning of the movement of the Gentiles to Christ. In the desire of the Greeks to come and see Him, Jesus recognizes the first green blade of an abundant harvest. With His Passion looming on the horizon, Jesus announces, "When I am lifted up from the earth, I will draw everyone to myself" (Jn 12:32). Jesus on the Cross is love lifted up for all to see. Love undying in the face of death. Love unrelenting in the face of hatred. The very love of God for us revealed. It is the love that draws all people to salvation.

The death of Jesus on the Cross was "a stumbling block to the Jews and foolishness to the Gentiles... but the power of God and the wisdom of God" (1 Cor 1:23-24). The mustard seed itself helps us understand that wisdom. The mustard seed is small. Yet, when bruised and broken, it gives forth its fiery vigor. A good image of Jesus. He is the mustard seed from whose bruised and broken body on the Cross the fire of God's love and power is unleashed in the world.

When Jesus tells His disciples the parable of the Mustard Seed, His disciples listen in wonder. A common garden vegetable, a plant that sprouts up to a mighty shrub welcoming all, now a symbol of the kingdom of God! This image overturns their way of thinking. God's greatness is found in the common, ordinary realities of this world. His kingdom is hidden in the lives of the disenfranchised. And, when it reaches its maturity, the oppressed are free, the outcast welcome, and the meek in possession of the land.

According to an ancient legend, the Persian king Darius once sent Alexander the Great a barrel of sesame seeds to acquaint him with the multitude of his soldiers. In return, Alexander sent a bag of mustard seeds to inform him of the fire and courage of his soldiers. A beautiful image for those enlisted in the service of Christ. Every faithful disciple courageously lives out the mustard seed principle embodied in Christ Himself. Not lording over others, but courageously dying to self and humbly serving others.

In every age, the parable of the Mustard Seed remains a challenge for the Church. The Church is not a kingdom of this world. The arrogance of political power and the desire to dominate bring her no increase. She is the seed, the humble grain, buried in the ground. When the Church is meek and serving others, she is true to herself.

During His public ministry, when Jesus was announcing the arrival of the kingdom of God, His own chosen apostles were constantly wondering who would be the greatest among them in that kingdom. They were elbowing each other out to sit one at His right and another at His left in power.

In the very days of the infant Church, this same childish behavior reared its ugly head both among the leaders and the members of the community. Some wanted prestige, fame, and power so much so that Peter, whom Jesus had named His vicar on earth, felt compelled to address the situation.

To the leaders of the Church, Peter gave this admonition:

"I exhort the presbyters among you, as a fellow presbyter myself and a witness to the sufferings of Christ and as one who has shared in the glory that is to be revealed. Be shepherds of the flock of God that has been entrusted to your care. Watch over it, not as a duty, but willingly, in accord with the will of God, not for sordid gain, but because you are eager to do so. Do not lord it over those in your charge, but be examples to the flock." *1 Pet 5:1-3*

And to the members of the community, he said:

"And all of you should clothe yourselves with humility in your relationships with one another, for 'God opposes the proud but he gives grace to the humble.'"
1 Pet 5:5

Only when the Church, that is, all her members, live in humility and self-sacrificing service, does God's kingdom grow in this world as a home for all.

CHAPTER 4

The Parable of the Wheat and Weeds

While the emperor Nero was living a life of luxury and sexual debauchery, killing family members and political opponents, the apostles Peter and Paul were preaching Jesus' gospel of love and mercy. While Hitler was systematically herding millions of Jews and others into concentration camps to die, Mother Teresa was caring for the outcasts on the streets of Calcutta. While Stalin was brutally slaughtering twenty million people, Mahatma Gandhi was promoting non-violence in a campaign for his country's independence. When the Cambodian leader Pol Pot was destroying his own people, Pope John Paul II was visiting Poland, building up the spirit of his home country.

At any point in history, the good and the bad live together in this world. Evil struggling to overtake the good. The malicious persecuting the virtuous. In the parable of the Wheat and the Weeds, Jesus explains this uncomfortable coexistence of good and evil.

> He then proposed another parable to them. "The kingdom of heaven may be compared to a man who sowed good seed in his field. While everyone was asleep, his enemy came, sowed weeds among the wheat, and then went away. When the wheat sprouted and ripened, the weeds also appeared.
>
> "The owner's servants came to him and asked, 'Master, did you not sow good seed in your field? Where then did these weeds come from?' He answered, 'one of my enemies has done this.' The servants then asked him, 'Do you want us to go and pull up the weeds?'

The Parable of the Wheat and Weeds

"He replied, 'No, because in gathering the weeds you might uproot the wheat along with them. Let them grow together until harvest. At harvest time I will tell the reapers, "Collect the weeds first and tie them in bundles to be burned. Then gather the wheat into my barn."'" *Mt 13:24-30*

This parable is found in Matthew's gospel. It is not in Luke's. However, Mark does record a parable which bears a striking resemblance to the parable of the Wheat and Weeds in Matthew. It is much simpler than the parable in Matthew. And, whereas Matthew provides an explanation of the parable in his gospel, Mark does not.

[Jesus] said, "The kingdom of God is like this; a man scatters seed on the ground. Night and day while he sleeps and while he is awake, the seed sprouts and grows, though he does not understand how. The ground produces fruit of its own accord —first the shoot, then the ear, then the full grain in the ear. And when the crop is ripe, he immediately stretches out the sickle, because the time for harvest has come." *Mk 4:26:29*

This is one of the most cryptic parables in Mark. Like other seed parables, it contrasts the scattering of the seed with the rich and abundant harvest that it produces. Jesus' point in this parable is not too hard to discern. The kingdom of God, seeded and planted in the ministry of Jesus, is at work mysteriously growing toward a good harvest.

Jesus makes the point that "of its own accord the land yields fruit." The seed grows independent of the farmer's efforts. It grows even when the farmer sleeps. The harvest is not the result of human work. The kingdom of God does not depend primarily on human activity. The growth of the kingdom of God in this world is grace. It is God's doing. Paul clearly taught this. He said,

> I planted the seed, and Apollos watered it, but God caused it to grow. So neither the one who plants nor the one who waters is of any importance but only God who causes the growth. *1 Cor 3:6*

From his own conversion on the road to Damascus, Paul personally understood the gift character of the kingdom. The rich harvest is a gift of God's grace. Therefore, we should never flatter ourselves into thinking that the success of God's work depends on us.

God longs for our cooperation, but our indifference and even our sins cannot stop the coming of His kingdom. God's kingdom is growing mysteriously among us. Its growth takes place even while we sleep. Many Jewish people in the first century were expecting the kingdom to come with fire and brimstone, with power and majesty. Jesus many times had to tell them that this is not how it was going to happen. They needed to be patient with God's unobtrusive ways.

Patience is waiting and trusting in God when we see no results. It is not passive. That is indolence. Rather, patience is the virtue that keeps us going when the going is no longer easy. "Perhaps there is only one cardinal sin: impatience. Because of impatience we were driven out of Paradise, because of impatience we cannot return" (W.H. Auden).

At the very end of the parable as found in Mark, Jesus hints at the final judgment. "And when the grain is ripe, he wields the sickle at once, for the harvest has come." This image Jesus takes from the prophet Joel who says:

> Wield the sickles, for the harvest is ripe; come and trample the grapes, for the winepress is full. The vats overflowing, for great is their wickedness.
> *Joel 4:13*

The Parable of the Wheat and Weeds

In his prophecy, Joel crowds together the two images of reaping the ripe grain and treading the mature grapes. He wants to intensify his message of the coming judgment of the nations. The prophet's strong language points to the final judgment when all the nations and all individuals will receive recompense for their deeds. God determined from all eternity the moment when creation would begin. He also fixed the hour of its judgment. Human life is fleeting. One brief moment, then judgment and eternity!

The parable as recorded for us by Mark places its emphasis on grace. God Himself is ushering in His kingdom on earth. Through Jesus' ministry, He is inviting all to enter. This stress on grace and generous welcome, the terseness of the parable and the lack of explanation are all hallmarks of Jesus' teaching. Thus, listening to the parable as recorded in Mark, we can be sure we are hearing the authentic voice of the Master.

When we open the gospel of Matthew and read the parable of the Wheat and Weeds, it sounds at first very much like Mark's parable of the seed growing secretly. Both parables compare the kingdom of heaven to a man planting a seed. Both emphasize the seed's secret growth, while the man is fast asleep. And both parables depict the coming judgment with the image of a harvest. But there are significant differences.

In the parable in Matthew's gospel, we hear about an enemy sowing weeds at night, servants wondering where the weeds came from, and reapers separating the weeds from the wheat and then burning the weeds. All these elements are added; and, they are allegorical. While we cannot say that Jesus did not speak allegorically at times, it is more probable that the simpler parable in Mark is the original.

Matthew himself, or someone else before him, may have added the allegorical details and their interpretation to the original parable as told by Jesus. In no way does this lessen the inspiration of the text. The whole process of passing on the words of Jesus from His lips to the written text of the gospels was under the divine inspiration of the Holy Spirit. The gospels may not always record the *ipssima verba Christi*, but they always give us the *ipssima vox Christi*.

In the parable in Matthew's gospel, Jesus speaks of weeds (ζιζάνια). The word is sometimes translated as "darnel" or "tares." This weed grows to almost two feet tall. Because it looks like the wheat, it is also called "false wheat." It is a poisonous weed. If eaten, it causes dizziness and nausea. It looks just like wheat until the harvest. Like thorns and thistles, darnel was a nuisance to the farmer of ancient times.

In the parable, when the servants see so many weeds growing among the wheat, they are surprised. They questioned the owner. Did he not plant good seed? Seeing the vast quantity of weeds, the owner himself immediately realizes that this is not the hand of Mother Nature. He tells the servants, "An enemy has done this." Someone is deliberately trying to destroy his work. It is an act of subversion meant to ruin his farm.

At this point in the story, the listeners would be expecting the owner in the parable to tell his servants to clear his field so that the weeds no longer have a chance to drain the soil of its nutrients, thus allowing the wheat to grow strong. But Jesus catches His listeners off guard. He tells them, "Let them grow together until harvest; then at harvest time I will say to the harvesters, 'First collect the weeds and tie them in bundles for burning; but gather the wheat into my barn.'"

The Parable of the Wheat and Weeds

The owner's unexpected response shows how concerned he is for the wheat. He does not want a single blade of wheat injured by uprooting the weeds. Furthermore, the owner's response emphasizes his patience. He is willing to wait until harvest. No rush to judgment. Patience. A needed virtue in our age of instant communication and immediate satisfaction.

Gifted with reason, we are wired to make judgments. We have the ability to discern the good from the bad, the beautiful from the ugly, the right from the wrong, and virtue from vice. This ability is an essential part of our being human. However, each judgment we make must be founded on truth not rumor, on fact not fiction, on substance and not on appearance. We must always temper our judgments with compassion. "Any fool can criticize, complain, and condemn—and most fools do. But it takes character and self-control to be understanding and forgiving" (Dale Carnegie). To rush to judge another is to condemn oneself!

Only at the harvest time comes the judgment. Then will the weeds and the wheat be separated. The wheat will be collected and stored in the owner's barn. The weeds bundled and burned! This graphic image echoes the eschatological teaching of John the Baptist.

To the many Pharisees and Sadducees who had come to the Jordan, John had announced the imminent coming of the Messiah. He thundered the warning: "His winnowing fan is in his hand. He will clear his threshing floor and gather his wheat into his barn, but the chaff he will burn with unquenchable fire" (Mt 3:12). When Jesus came as the Messiah, He deferred this fiery judgment announced by John to the end of the world. In His ministry, He brought forgiveness and mercy. This took everyone by surprise, even John the Baptist.

In Matthew's gospel, after telling the parable of the Wheat and the Weeds, Jesus tells two other parables. Then, He dismisses the crowds. He retires to the house to be alone with His disciples. Once inside Peter's house in Capernaum, the headquarters of His Galilean ministry, the disciples ask Jesus to explain the parable of the Wheat and the Weeds. They needed further instruction to comprehend the deep truths that Jesus is offering and they are unafraid to ask for it.

Jesus readily responds to their honest request. "For everyone who asks, receives..." (Lk 11:10). Jesus will never deny us when we ask for what is good for us. He offers to His questioning disciples and to us the following explanation of the parable.

> The one who sows good seed is the Son of Man. The field is the world, and the good seed stands for the children of the kingdom. The weeds are the children of the evil one, and the enemy who sowed them is the devil. The harvest is the end of the world, and the reapers are angels. Just as weeds are collected and burned in the fire, so will it be at the end of the world. The Son of Man will send forth his angels, and they will gather out of his kingdom all who cause sin and all whose deeds are evil. They will throw them into the fiery furnace, where there will be weeping and gnashing of teeth. Then the righteous will shine like the sun in the kingdom of their Father. He who has ears to hear, let him hear.
>
> Mt 13:37-43

Jesus explains the parable in simple, short sentences. The whole world (κόσμος—kosmos) is *the field* in the parable. The sower is the *Son of Man*. In the gospels, Jesus uses this title "the Son of Man" when He speaks of

Himself. Thus, Jesus is the one who sows or plants good people in the world. These are the people who hear His gospel and live it.

But Jesus' own ministry is limited in time and place. As He tells His disciples, "I was sent only to the lost sheep of the house of Israel" (Mt 15:24). It is His disciples who will bring the word of God outside the narrow confines of Galilee and Judea and continue the Son of Man's working of sowing good people in the world.

In Jesus' last appearance to His disciples in Matthew's gospel, the Risen Lord gives the Great Commission. He says,

> "Go, therefore, and make disciples of all nations, baptizing them in the name of the Father, and of the Son, and of the Holy Spirit, and teaching them to observe all that I have commanded you. And behold, I am with you always, to the end of the world."
>
> *Mt 28:19-20*

Jesus is with His disciples, working through them to bring the word of God into the whole world. Jesus sees the work of the disciples after His Ascension not as their work, but as His work of sowing the good seed of the children of the kingdom. Jesus is responsible for sowing "the sons of the kingdom" throughout the world and in His Church. Salvation is Jesus' work.

In telling the parable of the Wheat and the Weeds, Jesus is stretching His eyes beyond the beginnings of the Church. He is looking beyond the small group of individuals listening to Him preach. He sees people of every nation and race hearing His word through the ministry of the Church. And, Jesus recognizes that, within that community of faith in every age, there will be wheat and weeds. There will be those whose faith in His word makes them *children of the kingdom*. And, there will be others who reject His gospel and are *children of the evil one*.

It is only at the harvest time that the wheat and weeds are seen for what they are. Until then, both seem green and promising. Side by side, they promise a bountiful harvest. But appearances are deceptive. "Take nothing on its looks; take everything on evidence. There's no better rule" (Charles Dickens). At the final judgment, the evidence of charity, kindness, and faith will reveal the difference between the righteous and unrighteous among us.

Jesus does not hide the stark reality of a Church that embraces saints and sinners. He clearly places the blame of sin and evil on the devil. Satan is the sower of the weeds. He is the enemy who plants sinners in the world and in the Church. But his work is in vain. As Jesus reminds us, "Every plant that my heavenly Father has not planted will be uprooted" (Mt 15:13).

The devil knows where to plant the weeds. In the places of influence in society. In politics. In medicine. In schools and universities. In the entertainment world and the media. In the courts. And, even in the Church.

Satan is able to enlist in His service those who do His bidding. Politicians who place partisan politics over the common good. Doctors who become dealers in death. Entertainers who promote immoral behavior. Teachers, professors, and news persons who turn from the truth. Judges who pervert justice. And clergy and religious who fail in their commitment to serve unselfishly.

The devil hates goodness. He keeps moving the moral standards of our day further and further from the Ten Commandments. And all the while, we sleep.

Satan is the culprit responsible for the weeds among the wheat. He entices us to sin. God does allow the devil to tempt us, not to have us sin, but to strengthen our resolve and form our character. When we struggle with trials and temptations, we should not lose heart. "In this [we] rejoice, even if now for a little while [we] must suffer trials of many kinds. Thus, the genuine quality of [our]faith, which is more valuable than gold that is perishable even if it has been tested by fire, may be proved worthy of praise, glory, and honor when Jesus Christ is revealed" (1 Pet 1:6-7).

As Paul reminds us, "God is faithful and he will not allow you to be tried beyond your strength. But together with the trial he will also provide a way out and the strength to bear it" (1 Cor 10:13). In this verse, Paul is speaking of God's overarching providence. Yet, at the same time, the great Apostle of the Gentiles is clearly affirming the doctrine of free will.

God created us as rational beings. He has conferred on us the dignity of controlling our own actions. "God willed that man should be 'left in the hand of his own counsel,' so that he might of his own accord seek his Creator and freely attain his full and blessed perfection by cleaving to him" (*Catechism of the Catholic Church*, 1730).

God is wise. He never lets us be tempted beyond our strength. God allows us to be placed in certain circumstances where our virtue is put to the test. He directly wills us to use those moments as opportunities to grow closer to Him. When we look only to ourselves, we fall. But God is faithful; and, when we turn to Him, He will lead us through temptation to a greater holiness. "A man may lose the good things of this life against his will; but if he loses the eternal blessings, he does so with his own consent" (St. Augustine).

The devil who sows the weeds among the wheat is an intruder. He trespasses on another's property when the owner is sleeping. Satan hates the light. Satan is subtle and full of malice. Secrecy and dishonesty are his trademarks. Jesus presents the devil for what he is: a deceiver and a liar. "For even Satan masquerades as an angel of light" (2 Cor 11:14). He promises happiness, but leaves us empty and unfulfilled.

Satan imitates the work of Jesus. He does not sow thorns or thistles among the good wheat. Rather, he sows a counterfeit wheat. Something that looks like the real thing, but is not. This is his usual way of deceiving us. He deceives us into seeing something evil as good. He clothes vice in the vesture of virtue. He disguises license to do as one pleases as true freedom. But such unbridled self-satisfaction always entails the loss of freedom and slavery to sin.

For many in our world today, the devil is a vestige of unscientific age, a mere metaphor for human depravity. However, the reality of the devil belongs to the bedrock of Christian tradition. Even a casual reading of the New Testament brings us face to face with the devil. Within the gospel tradition, casting out the devil (exorcism) stands out as one of the miracles which Jesus most frequently performed. In fact, in the Gospel of Mark, exorcisms are the largest number of healings Jesus worked (Mk 1:21-28; 5:1-20; 7:24-30; and 9:14-29).

So integral to the ministry of Jesus were His exorcisms that, when the gospel writers wish to summarize His ministry, they do not fail to mention His exorcisms (Mk 1:32-34. 39, 3:11; Lk 7:21 and 13:32). Even other exorcists found Jesus' name effective to cast out the devil (Mk 9:38-41; Acts 19:13-20). Jesus' opponents likewise recognized the fact of His exorcisms. But they tried to discredit them by saying that He was in league with Satan himself (Mk 3:22).

The Parable of the Wheat and Weeds

So grounded in history was the memory of Jesus' casting out the devil that even the rabbis remembered it (*Sanhedrin*, 43a).

Jesus shared with His disciples His authority to cast out demons. "He summoned his twelve disciples and gave them authority over unclean spirits, with the power to drive them out and to cure every kind of disease and illness" (Mt 10:1; cf. Mk 3:15). And they did! They went about "casting out many demons, and they anointed with oil many sick people and cured them" (Mk 6:13). At Philippi, Paul himself cast out a demon from a slave girl (Acts 16:16-18).

From her earliest days at the time of the apostles, the Church continued Jesus' work of casting out the devil. Her mission, like His, is to rescue the world from the powers of darkness and ushering in the kingdom of God. In our day, the Church continues this work by preaching the gospel, celebrating the sacraments, and accomplishing works of charity.

The devil is real. Make no mistake about it! Evil is real. And, every individual needs to confront the power of evil and move away from the spiritual dominion of the devil. For, when the end of the world comes, there will be the final judgment and the angels will separate the good from the bad. They will divide into two groups those who belong to Jesus and those who have placed themselves under Satan's dominion by their sinful lives.

In the parable, Jesus speaks of *the end of the age* as the harvest. In both apocalyptic and rabbinic writings, this expression means the end of this present order. This is the first time that Jesus speaks of the end of the age in Matthew's gospel. The word "end" here is the Greek word συντελεία (sunteleia). This word is more accurately rendered "completion." It is not the annihilation of the created universe, but its transformation. It is God reigning glorious over all that He has created. It is the end of Satan's power.

The end of the world is, therefore, not something to fear, but to joyfully await. History is inexorably moving to the fulfillment of God's plan to bring us to Paradise. Thus, "we await our blessed hope, the appearance of the glory of our great God and Savior Jesus Christ" (Tit 2:13).

In the parable of the Wheat and the Weeds, Jesus speaks of the angels as instruments of God's judgment. This was a common image in apocalyptic literature. In the Book of Enoch (160 B.C.) and Revelation, the last book of the New Testament, God uses angels at the end of time to punish the evildoers and to save the just. Just as the reapers gather wheat into the barn and cast the weeds into the fire, the angels will usher the just into the kingdom of the Father and cast the evildoers into hell.

In the time of Jesus, rabbinic tradition was already describing hell as a furnace of fire. For example, the Book of Enoch says, "the names [of the wicked] shall be blotted out from the book of life...and they shall cry and make lamentation...in the fire they shall burn" (Enoch, 108). Today many reject hell as a fiery place of punishment. But this image would not have struck Jesus' audiences as strange. It was part of their religious world view.

The ultimate fate of the evildoers will be in stark contrast to that of the righteous. The evildoers will wail and grind their teeth in utter despair. The just will be clothed in glory. Jesus says that, "the righteous will shine like the sun in the kingdom of their Father." With this image, Jesus is alluding to the prophet Daniel.

The Parable of the Wheat and Weeds

> Many of those shall awake who sleep in the dust of the earth.
> Some shall gain everlasting life;
> others will earn shame and everlasting disgrace.
> However, the wise will shine like the brightness of the heavens, and those who lead many to righteousness
> will be as bright as the stars forever.   *Dan 12:2-3*

At the end of time, the scales of justice will be balanced. From the dawn of our moral life, the law of justice is inviolably woven in all our thoughts and actions. Every voluntary act awaits a just recompense. The divine Judge will come and reward each of us as we deserve. "Behold, I am coming soon, and I will bring with me my reward to repay everyone as his deeds deserve" (Rev 22:12).

Ultimately, we are all accountable not to the majority but to God. In his day, Daniel Webster was well-respected for his moral character. Once asked what thought most occupied his mind, he replied, "The fact of my personal accountability to God." How different our world would be if each of us thought this way!

In writing his gospel, Matthew painfully knew that the Church was a community of both sinners and saints. Some strictly observed all that they were taught. Others were lax. There were even some individuals pretending to be prophets, all the while seeking their own honor and personal gain (Mt 7:15). In retelling Jesus' parable of the Wheat and Weeds, Matthew is directly addressing this mixed situation before his eyes.

To those questioning how to deal with a community less than perfect, Matthew offers Jesus' parable of the Wheat and Weeds. It is not for us to divide the Church into the good and the bad, the saint and the sinner. It is not up to us to decide who deserves punishment and who does not. Jesus Himself will do that at the end of time. "No one can take to himself the ensign of Christ...[and be] judge of others before the day of judgment. If the Church has been already purified, what do we reserve for the Lord" (St. Jerome).

Jesus concludes His explanation of the parable of the Wheat and Weeds with the challenge, "Whoever has ears ought to hear." He uses this same expression at the end of the parable of the Sower and the Seed and the parable about the salt that loses its flavor. This expression echoes the words the prophet Ezekiel places on the lips of God Himself.

> But when I have spoken to you I will open your mouth, and you will say to them, "This is what the Lord God said: 'If anyone wishes to listen, he may listen. If anyone refuses to listen, he may refuse. For they are a rebellious house.'" *Ezek 3:27*

By using this expression "Whoever has ears ought to hear," Jesus emphasizes His divine authority. He is more than just explaining a parable. He is uttering a prophecy. He is placing on us the imperative to hear His words and put them into action.

In conclusion, we need to remember the true nature of the Church. The Church as founded by Jesus is a divine institution. But we who are members of the Church are human. There is a basic human goodness in each of us. But our goodness is brittle. It is tainted by pride, jealousy, lust, and so many hidden vices. As Jesus willingly gives us time to change, we must do likewise with each other. Jesus is eager to heal us of the poison of sin. He wants us to grow to fullness of charity so that He may gather us together in Paradise.

CHAPTER 5

The Parable of the Two Sons

The *Mona Lisa* is the most visited work in the Louvre Museum in Paris. Leonardo da Vinci spent years trying to capture in this work the enigmatic thoughts of Lisa Gheradini (La Gioconda), the wife of a local aristocrat. For 500 years, admirers have scrutinized her smile, trying to uncover the painting's secret. In 2015, French scientist Pascal Cotte, using reflective light technology, discovered an earlier portrait hidden underneath the surface of the painting. This was a "first draft" that da Vinci used to create his most celebrated masterpiece.

The most famous works of art did not jump spontaneously from the brush of the masters. Exactly the opposite. Great artists first did sketches and rough drafts of their works and labored hard at perfecting them. From the hands of Michelangelo, there exist at least 600 drawings and sketches that reveal the time and energy he put into his works.

Arguably, the parable of the Prodigal Son is the most famous of all the parables Jesus told. The 19th century novelist and social critic Charles Dickens described it as "the finest short story ever written." With much creative reflection, Jesus framed His teaching of God's mercy in this unforgettable portrait of a father's love for two sons who both disappointed him. It is not unreasonable to imagine Jesus' first sketching these images and then later refining them. In fact, in Matthew's gospel, the following parable of the Two Sons very much resembles such a rough draft.

A man had two sons. He went to the first and said, "My son, go and work in the vineyard today." He answered, "I will not," but later he had a change of heart and went. The father then gave the same instruction to the second son, who answered, "Of course I will," but then did not go. Which of the two complied with his father's instructions? They responded, "The first." Then Jesus said to them, "Amen, I say to you, tax collectors and prostitutes are entering the kingdom of God ahead of you. For John came to show you the path of righteousness, but you did not believe him; whereas the tax collectors and prostitutes did. Yet even after you realized that, you still refused to change your minds and believe him." *Mt 21:28-32*

The parable of the Two Sons and the parable of the Prodigal Son have the same theme. They explore the wrong way sons relate to a father who loves them. Both parables begin in the same way: "A man had two sons" (Mt 21:28; Lk 15:11). In both parables when the father addresses his son directly, he uses the Greek word τέκνον (teknon). This word expresses affection and trust (Mt 21:28; Lk 15:31).

The parable of the Prodigal Son is twenty-two verses in Luke 15. The parable of the Two Sons is only five verses in Matthew 21. Many commentators have written much about the parable of the Prodigal Son. But they have said little about Matthew's brief parable of the Two Sons, a parable freighted with meaning.

Only Matthew records this parable. He is writing his gospel to a Jewish audience who are very interested in being righteous. Matthew speaks of righteousness more than twice as much as Luke. Righteousness throughout Sacred Scripture means the right relationship with God

The Parable of the Two Sons

and with others. His Jewish audience considered obedience to God the dividing mark between the righteous and the sinner.

Ordinary people in Jesus' day respected the apparent righteousness of the religious leaders. Because of their lack of education and their work, they could not think of themselves as matching the piety of the professional religious. Jesus uses this parable to overturn this inadequate understanding of righteousness.

First, let us look at the context of the parable of the Two Sons. On what occasion does Jesus tell this short parable? To whom does He address it? And, what is His purpose in relating this story? After answering these questions, we will be in a better position to look at the parable itself.

Jesus tells the parable of the Two Sons during the last week of His life. On Palm Sunday, Jesus' triumphal entrance into Jerusalem attracted the praise of the masses. It enkindled the furor of His enemies. Immediately, on entering the city, Jesus went straight to the Temple. Overturning the tables of the money changers and merchants, he angered the Temple leadership. He healed the blind and the lame and willingly accepted the hosanna of the children, acclaiming Him Messiah that day.

> When he entered the temple and began to teach, the chief priests and the elders of the people approached him and asked, "By what authority are you doing these things? And who gave you this authority?" *Mt 21:23*

Jesus' aggressive zeal in driving out the merchants and money changers and their consequent loss of revenue gall them. His claim to forgive sins exasperates them (Mt 9:6). His teaching infuriates them, "for he taught them as one having authority, and not as their scribes" (Mt 7:29). Skeptical of His mission, they demand His credentials.

This is not the first time that the leaders of the Jewish people demand Jesus' credentials. After seeing many of His miracles and witnessing His exorcisms, they wanted Jesus to show proof that He did this with God's authority (Mt 12:28; 16:1). Now, at the end of His life, their demand is ominous.

When John the Baptist began preaching and baptizing at the Jordan River, these same religious leaders wasted no time to inquire of his credentials. They sent priests and Levites to examine him. When he said that he was not the Messiah, they returned to Jerusalem satisfied (Jn 1:19). But, now that Jesus was teaching in the very heart of Judaism, they felt compelled to act. Their authority was in question.

Those demanding proof of Jesus' authority are the highest religious authorities in Jerusalem. The next time Jesus meets them will be when He is dragged in before them to be judged (Mt 26:47-57). At this moment, they are seeking to trap Him and prepare their case against Him. Only scribes legitimately trained had the authority to teach publicly. If Jesus says that He is teaching on His own authority or if He claims to have divine authority, in either case, they would be able to begin legal proceedings against Him.

In such a hostile situation, Jesus does not address them directly. He seeks to diffuse their anger by asking them a question.

> Jesus said to them in reply, "I will ask you one question. If you give me an answer, then I will tell you by what authority I do these things. Where did John's baptism originate? From heaven or from men?" They argued among themselves. *Mt 21: 24-25*

John's memory was held in high esteem. All the people acknowledged him as a prophet. The religious leaders dare not demean his reputation. If Jesus' adversaries admit that John had his authority from God, then they would be forced to accept Jesus' authority, since John himself on more than one occasion had indicated that Jesus was the Messiah sent by God.

Trapped by Jesus' question, they consult with each other. They are looking for a way to avoid the truth. They want to protect their own self-interest and not lose face before the people. So they profess ignorance. A weak subterfuge! Judging situations through our interests and not honestly destroys our character. "The virtues are lost in self-interest as rivers are lost in the sea" (Franklin D. Roosevelt). Only the courageous can face the truth.

The answer that Jesus' adversaries make to His question conceals their deliberate resistance to what God had done in the Baptist and what God was doing in Jesus. Their false claim of ignorance undermines their own claim to lead others in the way of salvation. Jesus responds to them with the parable of the Two Sons. He confronts them with the truth about themselves.

In the parable, a man owns a vineyard. On a day when he needs to have work done, he approaches his two sons. The fact that he sends his sons with the order to go immediately indicates it is harvest time and the need is urgent.

The owner addresses them as τέκνον, (teknov: son or child). This is an intimate term of endearment. It is not a word that the owner would have spoken to his servants. These are his very own children whom he loves and cares for. The father does not ask the sons to go into the vineyard. He sends them: "Son, go out and work in the vineyard." He is not asking them to go. He is commanding them.

The first son responds immediately to his father, "I will not!" He is curt, disrespectful, and rude. He is too self-centered, too absorbed in his own affairs, to even entertain his father's command. The second son is much more respectful. He does not hesitate. His answer sounds like the quick response of a soldier to his officer's command. He literally says, "Yes, sir!" However, the second son does not go into the vineyard. But the first son does.

The first son changes his mind. The Greek word μεταμεληθεὶς (metameletheis) indicates regret. He realizes he should have spoken otherwise and, regretting his disrespect, he obeys his father. He goes into the vineyard to work. Love is always an action. "If you love me, you will keep my commandments" (Jn 14:15). Deeds speak louder than words. "Well done is better than well said" (Benjamin Franklin).

The second son is more disrespectful than his brother. He says he will go to work in the vineyard, but he does not go. He does not do as his father commanded him. Mere intention is useless. The way to hell is paved with good intentions.

The father has great affection for his second son, but the son has no great love of his father. The father addresses him with a term of endearment. But he addresses his father in a formal, authoritarian way as "Sir." The second son sees his father as a master and himself as his servant. This is the very same attitude of the elder brother in the parable of the Prodigal Son.

When Jesus asks His adversaries which of the two sons did their father's will, they know what to answer. Jewish society was duty-oriented, not rights-oriented. In commercial undertakings, rights were safely guarded. But, in the family, everyone knew their obligations. A father had to care for his family; and, he had the unquestionable right to be respected and obeyed. When asked, a son was expected to let go of his own plans immediately and help his father in his need.

Jesus' adversaries give the right answer. But, in so doing, they actually accuse themselves. Jesus has skillfully set up the parable so that the chief priests and the elders stand exposed for their own hypocrisy. They acknowledge that doing the father's will is what matters, not just voicing obedience. In the character of the second son who does not listen to his father, Jesus paints their portrait.

In *Hamlet*, Shakespeare's most famous tragedy, Hamlet holds up a mirror to his mother, the queen.

> Come, Come, and sit you down; you shall not budge.
> You go not until I set you up a glass
> Where you may see the inmost part of you.
> *Hamlet:* 3.4.19-21

Peering in the mirror, the queen shudders at what she sees and cries out,

> Thou turn'st mine eyes into my very soul, And there I see such black and grainèd spots as will not leave their tinct. *Hamlet:* 3.4.89-91

The parable of the Two Sons is the mirror that Jesus holds up to his adversaries. They see themselves reflected back in the image of the son who does not do the father's will.

In condemning the second son for not doing the father's will, they are condemning themselves. Like him, they honor God with their lips, but their deeds are far from him (Mt 15:8). By their words, they profess loudly that they are doing what God wants. But, when God calls them to a conversion of heart and to "the obedience of faith" (Rom 1:5) through the preaching of the Baptist and the ministry of Jesus, they do not obey.

Jesus ends the parable of the Two Sons by saying, "Amen, I say to you, tax collectors and prostitutes are entering the kingdom of God ahead of you" (Mt 21:31). On other occasions, Jesus uses the same expression "I say to you" to bring a parable to its conclusion. Thus, He concludes the parable of the Great Supper (Lk 14:24), the parable of the Lost Sheep (Lk 15:7), the parable of the Lost Coin (Lk 15:10), and the parable of the Pharisee and the Publican (Lk 18:14).

Jesus has confronted the chief priests and elders of the people with the painful truth about themselves. As leaders of God's Chosen People, they are steeped in the knowledge of divine revelation. They should have been the first to have listened and obeyed the call of the Baptist to repent and the call of Jesus to enter the kingdom of God. But, because of their pride and self-interest, they did not. By their own willful disobedience, they forfeit their authority as leaders.

The parable of the Two Sons ends at verse 31 without a condemnation hurled at these leaders. Jesus leaves it to them to acknowledge their own sin of disobedience. Jesus ends the parable on a note of hope. He says, "Tax collectors and prostitutes are entering the kingdom of God before you" (Mt 21:31). He does not exclude His adversaries.

The Greek word προάγουσιν (proagousin) literally means "to go before" or "to lead the way forward or into." It is in the present tense. And so Jesus is telling these self-important leaders that the very sinners whom they so condescendingly spurned are accepting the gift of salvation. They are the true leaders, first to enter the

The Parable of the Two Sons

kingdom, while the self-professed leaders are plotting against Jesus.

Jesus leaves open the question whether or not they will follow after those who do the will of God and enter the kingdom. Like the elder son in the parable of the Prodigal Son, the chief priests and elders are standing outside the kingdom on the doorstep. The celebration has begun inside the kingdom of God. The door is still open for them to enter.

Jesus is most merciful. He has convicted them of sin. Yet, He has not condemned them. We should never put a limit on God's mercy. "God's mercy is so great that you may sooner drain the sea of its water, or deprive the sun of its light, or make space too narrow than diminish the great mercy of God" (Charles Spurgeon).

To the parable as originally spoken by Jesus, Matthew adds the following words:

> For John came to show you the path of righteousness, but you did not believe him; whereas the tax collectors and prostitutes did. Yet even after you realized that, you still refused to change your minds and believe in him. *Mt 21:32*

Luke records this very same saying of Jesus. But he places it in the context of Jesus' testimony to John the Baptist (Lk 7:28-30). Most likely, this was an authentic saying of Jesus preserved in tradition. Matthew and Luke did not discard it. They placed it where it best served their purpose to expose the patronizing attitude of those who demanded proof of Jesus' mission.

By placing this independent saying after the parable of the Two Sons, Matthew makes explicit what is implicit in the parable itself. The leaders who claimed obedience to God's revelation refused His word spoken through

John. And, when God gives them His Word, Jesus, they likewise turn away. They witness sinners convert and are not moved. They remain hardened in their hearts. For not accepting God's word and for not recognizing the working of His grace in sinners, they stand doubly judged and condemned.

As we read the parable today, can we not see in the two sons two types of people? Is not the parable a line dividing the truly righteous and the self-righteous? "The whole of human history is marked by the original fault freely committed by our first parents" (*Catechism of the Catholic Church*, 390). Thus, all need to be saved by Jesus. Some sinners hear the gospel, let it sink in, accept it with their heart, confess their sins and are changed. They are the first son in the parable.

Others never face the truth about themselves. They delude themselves into thinking that their actions make them pleasing to God. They are blind to their own sins and do not obey God's call to repent. They never fully accept Christ as Savior. They never take up their work in his vineyard, the Church. They are the second son in the parable.

In telling the parable and leaving the door open to His adversaries, Jesus is extending His arms to welcome all. Whether we are the first son or the second son, Jesus looks at us with love. He is ready to forgive us and welcome us into His kingdom today.

The parable of the Two Sons also contains an implicit Christology. In the parable, there are two sons. Neither one is perfect in responding to the father. One fails in word and then responds in deed. The other responds in word and fails in deed. But implied in the parable is another son. This son, by contrast, accepts the father's authority. He always says "yes" and goes into the vineyard to do the will of the father. This third son implied in the parable is Jesus Himself!

From the first moment of the Incarnation, on entering the world, the Son of God says, "As is written of me in the scroll, 'behold, I come to do your will, O God'" (Heb 10:7). Jesus lived His whole life in total obedience to the Father's will. During His public ministry, Jesus explained His mission the same way. He said, "The one who sent me is with me. He has not left me alone, because I always do what is pleasing to him" (Jn 8:29; 5:30; 6:38). Jesus had the authority to accomplish the work of redemption, because He did the will of the Father who sent Him.

At the end of His life, in the shadows of Gethsemane, Jesus condenses His whole life of obedience to the Father into a single prayer. Accepting the Cross as God's way to redeem us sinners, Jesus cries out, "Father...not my will but yours be done" (Lk 22: 42). In obedience to the Father, Jesus dies on the Cross. Adam's disobedience had barred the gates of Paradise. By His obedience, Jesus, the Son of the God, opens for us the way to heaven. It is now ours to follow.

CHAPTER 6

The Parable of the Sheep and Goats

In the Kidron Valley in Jerusalem lies the largest and most important Jewish cemetery in the world. The Kidron Valley runs north to south dividing the eastern side of the Old City from the Mount of Olives. It is actually a dry river bed just below the eastern wall of the Temple Mount. It is crowded with tombs. Some date from the time of Jesus Himself.

According to Jewish belief, the Messiah is to appear in the Kidron Valley at the end of time. This is why many pious Jews have chosen to be buried there. They desire to be first in line for the resurrection on the last day.

Sacred Scripture indicates that the Last Judgment will take place in the Kidron Valley. The post-exilic prophet Joel had said that the final reckoning of humankind would take place in the Valley of Jehoshaphat:

> I will gather all the nations together
> and bring them down to the Valley of Jehoshaphat.
> There I shall bring them to judgment on behalf of
>   my people
> and my inheritance Israel. *Joel 4:2*

In popular tradition, the Kidron Valley is identified with the Valley of Jehoshaphat. The name "Jehoshaphat" means "the Lord judges." In the vision of the prophet Joel, the Lord is seated above this valley as He enters into judgment with the nations.

Many times in His public ministry, Jesus crossed over the Kidron Valley. Whether He was on His way to Jerusalem from Bethany, the home of Martha, Mary, and Lazarus, or leaving the city to return to their home,

The Parable of the Sheep and Goats

He would pass the tombs on either side of His path. Whenever Jesus stopped on the Mount of Olives either to pray or teach, His eyes would naturally come to rest on these tombs of those waiting for the Last Judgment. No surprise, then, that Jesus chose this place to give His most extensive teaching on the end times.

Jesus spent the final week of His life teaching in the Temple. Three days before His own death, when He is leaving the Temple, Jesus' disciples proudly point to the magnificent Temple built by Herod. It is glistening in the golden light of the setting sun and they are taken by its beauty. Jesus responds to their admiration of the Temple with His prophecy of its impending destruction: "Do you see all these things? Amen, I say to you, not one stone here will be left upon another; every one will be thrown down" (Mt 24:2).

After crossing the Kidron Valley, Jesus comes to the Mount of Olives. His disciples are curious about what Jesus had said about the final days. And so "the disciples came to him privately, saying, 'Tell us, when will this happen, and what will be the sign of your coming and of the end of the age?'" (Mt 24:3). Jesus sits down and responds to their two questions.

First, He speaks of the end of time (Mt 24:4-35). Then He talks about His second coming (Mt 24:36-25:30). Jesus' response, given privately to the disciples, is the longest answer Jesus gives to any question ever asked of Him. Matthew records Jesus' extensive teaching given on this occasion in Jesus' fifth discourse in his gospel (Mt 24:1—25:46).

In this last discourse of Jesus in Matthew's gospel, Jesus predicts the destruction of the Temple. He also speaks of the Parousia when He will return at the end of time. With the parable of the Ten Virgins (Mt 25:1-13), Jesus encourages His disciples to be ready for His return, whenever it may happen. With the parable of the Talents (Mt 25:14-30), Jesus exhorts them to be faithful to their duties until He returns, using their gifts to build up the kingdom. Then He speaks of the great judgment that will determine the eternal destiny of the nations.

When the Son of Man comes in his glory, and all the angels with him, then he will sit on the throne of his glory. All the nations will be gathered before him, and he will separate people one from another as a shepherd separates the sheep from the goats. He will place the sheep on his right and the goats on his left.

Then the King will say to those on his right, "Come, you who are blessed by my Father, inherit the kingdom prepared for you from the foundation of the world. For I was hungry and you gave me something to eat; I was thirsty and you gave me something to drink; I was a stranger and you welcomed me; I was naked and you clothed me; I was ill and you took care of me; I was in prison and you came to visit me."

Then the righteous will say to him, "Lord, when did we see you hungry and give you something to eat, or thirsty and give you something to drink? When did we see you a stranger and welcome you, or naked and clothe you? When did we see you ill or in prison and come to visit you?" And the King will answer, "Amen, I say to you, whatever you did for one of the least of these brethren of mine, you did for me."

Then he will say to those on his left, "Depart from me, you accursed, into the eternal fire prepared for the devil and his angels. For I was hungry and you did not give me anything to eat; I was thirsty

The Parable of the Sheep and Goats

and you did not give me anything to drink; I was a stranger and you did not welcome me; I was naked and you did not give me any clothing; I was ill and in prison and you did not visit me."

Then they will ask him, "Lord, when did we see you hungry or thirsty or a stranger or naked or ill or in prison and not minister to you?" He will answer them, "Amen, I say to you, whatever you failed to do for one of the least of these brethren of mine, you failed to do for me." And they will go away to eternal punishment, but the righteous will enter eternal life. *Mt 25:31-46*

How significant that Jesus speaks this parable on the Mount of Olives. It was from this very spot that Jesus rode down and across the valley into Jerusalem as the King of Peace on the Sunday before His death (Lk 19:28-44). It was from the Mount of Olives that He would ascend triumphant over death after the Resurrection (Acts 1:1-12). On this very same place, according to the prophet Zechariah, the judge of the world was to place His feet at the end of time (Zec 14:4).

Now, seated on the Mount of Olives, with the Valley of Jehoshaphat at His feet, Jesus reveals to His disciples in the parable of the Sheep and the Goats that He Himself will be the judge of all nations. At His first coming to earth, Jesus slipped quietly into the world under the obscurity of our humanity. At His second coming, Jesus will be seen by all in the glory of His divinity. He came among us in weakness and died in shame. He will come again in power and reign in glory.

In the parable of the Sheep and Goats, Jesus makes use of images from conventional Jewish apocalyptic thought, e.g., the coming of God at the end of time as judge of all, the resurrection of the dead, the presence of the angels executing God's judgment, the separation of the good and the bad, and the just recompense for both. In Jewish apocalyptic literature, God is always the judge. But, in this parable, Jesus presents Himself as the judge. He is the king and God is His Father. And each person is judged on the basis of their relationship with Jesus, albeit implicit in their care of the needy.

This is the last parable Jesus ever speaks. Its startling originality gives us every assurance that we are hearing the actual teaching of Jesus Himself at the end of His life. It is the final parable in Matthew's gospel with an image of the Last Judgement unique to Matthew alone.

In the parable, Jesus refers to Himself as the Son of Man. This is His favorite expression when speaking of Himself. Using this title in the parable, Jesus deliberately evokes the apocalyptic prophecy of Daniel about the end time.

While I was watching,
> thrones were set in place,
> and the Ancient One sat on his throne.

His robe was as white as snow,
> and the hair on his head was as pure as wool.

His throne was ablaze with fiery flames,
> and its wheels were a burning fire...

The court was in session,
> and the books lay open...

As the night visions continued,
> I beheld approaching on the clouds of heaven
> one like a son of man.

He came before the Ancient One
> and was presented to him.

Dominion and glory and kingship
> were conferred upon him
so that all peoples and nations of every language
> would become his servants.

The Parable of the Sheep and Goats

> His dominion is an everlasting dominion
>   that will never pass away,
> and his kingdom is one
>   that will never be destroyed.   *Dan 7:9-14*

This passage from Daniel is one of the most powerful in Sacred Scripture. Historically, Daniel is speaking about the coming of God to judge the evil ruler Antiochus Epiphanes and all those who, like him, persecute God's faithful people. God will sit in judgment, condemn, and destroy those evildoers. He will then establish His kingdom on earth, handing it over to the Son of Man. Daniel's words, however, go far beyond their historical context and give us a glimpse of the events of the end time.

In Daniel's prophecy, the figure of the Son of Man is both a collective and individual symbol. On the one hand, the Son of Man is all the faithful Jews destined to reign in God's kingdom. To those who had been so fiercely persecuted, power and authority will be given. On the other hand, the Son of Man is the Messiah who embodies in Himself God's power and sovereignty.

Of all the passages of Sacred Scripture, this passage from Daniel helped to shape Jesus' self-understanding. The final kingdom of God includes all God's faithful. But, just as the great mustard shrub is already in the tiny mustard seed, the kingdom of God is truly embodied in Jesus. In His healings and exorcisms is present the very power of God ushering in the kingdom. In the fullest sense, Jesus is the Son of Man prophesied by Daniel.

Jesus tells His disciples that, "when the Son of Man comes in his glory, and all the angels with him, he will sit upon his glorious throne, and all the nations will be assembled before him." This is the final moment when God will bring to completion the triumph of good over evil, thus establishing His eternal kingdom. People will be divided into two groups. The blessed will be given the place of honor on Jesus' right. On His left, the accursed. This will not be a trial. It will be the moment of sentencing. Jesus Himself, the Son of Man, will pronounce the sentence.

Over centuries, the right side has come to represent honor. The left side has come to symbolize disgrace. It seems that the distinction originally arose from the fact that most people were right-handed; and, they tended to think of left-handed people as sinister.

In Old Testament times, the most honored place next to a king was on his right. Ancient monarchs prided themselves on the number of wives in their harem. Hebrew kings were no exception (1 Ki 11:3). On the day of taking a new bride, the king would give her special honor by placing her on his right. In a song celebrating the Davidic king's marriage to a foreign princess, the psalmist says, "a princess arrayed in Ophir's gold comes to stand at your right hand" (Ps 45:10). Like their neighbors, the Israelites also held the mother of the king in great esteem. That is why Solomon placed a throne for his mother Bathsheba at his right (1 Ki 2:19).

Even the great Roman poet Virgil recognized the significance of right and left. He located the Elysian Fields, the place of the dead honored by the gods, to the right of the palace of Dis, the god of the underworld. And to the left, he placed Tartarus, the gigantic place of torment for the damned (Virgil, Aeneid, 6:540). For peoples of different cultures, the right side has consistently stood for goodness; the left, for evil.

Thus, when Jesus places the sheep on the right and the goats on His left, He is following the common understanding of the symbolism of right and left. He is also

The Parable of the Sheep and Goats

appealing to a particular custom of the Sanhedrin. At this Jewish court, two scribes would stand before the judge to record the sentences. The scribe on the right wrote the sentence for those acquitted. The scribe on the left, the sentence for those condemned.

In the parable, Jesus speaks of the righteous as sheep. An apt image. Sheep are docile. They represent simplicity and patience. They are profitable to their owner. The Scriptures consistently call God's chosen ones sheep. They belong to God who shepherds them and values them (Ps 100:3; Ps 74:1; Ps 23:1-6). The sheep are placed on the right.

The unrighteous, Jesus labels goats. Goats are unruly, naturally quarrelsome, and randy. They are less profitable to their owner than sheep. In fact, in the parable, Jesus uses the diminutive form of the word for goats. He calls them "kids" (ἐρίφια) to emphasize their worthlessness. The goats are placed on the left.

Even before the king speaks a word, the sheep and the goats are separated. Whether we are standing on the right or the left at the final judgment will be the inevitable result of our lives. The separation will be instantaneous and irrevocable. "We must all appear before the judgment seat of Christ, so that each one may receive recompense, according to what he did in the body, whether good or evil" (2 Cor 5:10). In the light of God's presence, we will immediately see ourselves as we truly are. Our own deeds will either condemn us or defend us.

In the parable, the king speaks first to the sheep. Jesus is more eager to bless than to curse, to reward than to punish. He tells them that the works of mercy which they had performed while on earth for the needy have merited them a place in heaven. Jesus is actually taking the practical works of charity from Isaiah 58:6-7 and Tobit 4:4-11 and making them the standard of judgment. How well Jesus knew the Scriptures of His own people!

Jesus' words astonish those on His right. They are surprised not by Jesus' reminding them of good deeds, but by the fact that He says that they were done to Him. He says to them, "For I was hungry and you gave *me* food, I was thirsty and you gave *me* drink, a stranger and you welcomed *me*, naked and you clothed *me*, ill and you cared for *me*, in prison and you visited *me*."

Equally stunned are those on Jesus' left. Jesus condemns them for not doing these very same works of mercy for those in need. Those on His left do not understand. They protest, "Lord, when did we see *you* hungry or thirsty or a stranger or naked or ill or in prison, and not minister to *your* needs?"

Both the righteous and unrighteous had no idea that caring for the needs of others was truly caring for Jesus. But Jesus says that it was. He says to them and to us, "Amen, I say to you, whatever you did for one of these least brothers of mine, you did for me."

With these words, Jesus proclaims His oneness with all those in need. In fact, after Adam and Eve's fall from grace, all their children were impoverished and left in need. The Son of God became one with us precisely so that He could enrich us with His divinity. "For you are well aware of the grace of our Lord Jesus Christ. Although he was rich, he became poor for your sake so that by his poverty you might become rich" (2 Cor 8:9).

As St. Athanasius, the great defender of the divinity of Jesus, taught, "the Son of God became man so that we might become God" (*De incarnatione* 54.3). And, as the 5th century Council of Chalcedon taught, Jesus is "con-

The Parable of the Sheep and Goats

substantial with the Father according to his Godhead, and consubstantial with us according to his Manhood." What ineffable love! What unutterable condescension to be so totally one with us! What complete identification with us!

Because of the mystery of the Incarnation, the Son of God, who took our flesh and blood as His very own, is not ashamed to call us His brothers and sisters (Heb 2:11). In fact, Jesus has given our human nature a dignity higher than that of the angels. Pope Saint Leo the Great beautifully expressed this when preaching on the Ascension of Jesus.

> The blessed apostles…had a great and inexpressible cause for joy when it saw man's nature rising above the dignity of the whole heavenly creation, above the ranks of angels, above the exalted status of archangels. Nor would there be any limit to its upward course until humanity was admitted to a seat at the right hand of the eternal Father, to be enthroned at last in the glory of him to whose nature it was wedded in the person of the Son.
> *Pope Saint Leo the Great*, Sermo 1 de Ascensione, 2-4

It is because of the Incarnation and Redemption that Jesus considers any service done to another as done to Him. He counts it of great value and reckons it as honoring Him, even when done unwittingly. So profound is Jesus' identification with us that when we love others in self-sacrificial service, attending to their needs, we are loving Jesus.

However, we should be careful how we interpret Jesus' standard of judgment in the parable of the Sheep and Goats. Jesus seems to be condemning the unrighteous solely for their sins of omission, that is, for not being attentive to the needy. No mention of idolatry, unbelief, murder, adultery, or gross injustice. Jesus seems to be ignoring these other sins that one would normally list as excluding the sinner from heaven (Gal 5:19-21; Eph 5:5; Rev 22:15).

On the one hand, by focusing on the corporal works of mercy in the parable, Jesus is certainly challenging us to pay close attention to these positive expressions of the supreme virtue of charity. On the other hand, He is by no means saying that every other sin does not matter. That would reduce the Christian faith to a mere "do-good and be-kind" religion. Hardly the ethical standard Jesus so consistently taught throughout His public ministry!

In sending out the disciples to preach, Jesus placed a very high value on the virtue of faith. He said, "Whoever acknowledges me before men, I will also acknowledge before my Father in heaven. But whoever denies me before men, I also will deny before my heavenly Father" (Mt 10:32-33). What we believe about Jesus matters. How we live out our beliefs matters.

The willingness to publicly stand for our Christian beliefs has eternal consequences. What a needed reminder at a time when it is convenient to divorce one's faith from one's political views. Today moral issues are argued in the media, debated in our legislatures, and decided in our courts. Silence for the believer is not an option! Not speaking out in favor of the truths about life and morality given us by Jesus makes us salt without flavor to be cast aside and trodden underfoot (Mt 5:13).

Furthermore, in the parable of the Talents, Jesus tells us that we will be judged by how well we use the gifts which He gives us for the service of others (Mt 25:14-30). Each one of us has been given the great gift of the gospel and the Church. Jesus expects us to share the gospel

The Parable of the Sheep and Goats

by word and deed. He wants us to help others enter the Church which He Himself founded as the ordinary means of salvation (Mt 28:16-20). We have been given so much and have a great responsibility to share our gifts. "Much will be demanded of the person to whom much has been given, and even more will be asked of a person to whom more has been entrusted" (Lk 12:48). In addition, the same compassion which God shows us in forgiving our sins, we are expected to show to one another (Mt 18: 21-35). In fact, when we pray the Our Father, we either bless or curse ourselves when we say, "forgive us our debts as we forgive our debtors" (Mt 6:12; Lk 11:4). If we refuse to forgive others, we are asking God not to forgive us. And, with sins unforgiven, we are certainly not fit to enter the kingdom of heaven (Rev 21:27).

When Jesus concluded His nighttime conversation with Nicodemus, He said, "Whoever believes in the Son has eternal life, whoever does not believe in the Son will not see life, but the wrath of God rests upon him" (Jn 3:36). When Jesus commissioned the eleven disciples at His Ascension, He instructed them saying, "Go forth into the whole world and proclaim the gospel to all creation. Whoever believes and is baptized will be saved; whoever does not believe will be condemned" (Mk 16:15-16). Paul taught that salvation comes from hearing the gospel and believing (Rom 10: 13-17). Clearly faith is necessary for salvation.

But what about those who never come to know Jesus? What about those who never hear the gospel? Are they forever condemned? The parable of the Sheep and the Goats provides the answer.

Jesus begins the parable by saying, "When the Son of Man comes in his glory, and all the angels with him, he will sit upon his glorious throne, and all the nations (πάντα τὰ ἔθνη: panta ta ethnē) will be assembled before him." The words "all the nations" can certainly be understood to mean everyone. But, almost without exception in Sacred Scripture, the word "nations" (τὰ ἔθνη: ta ethnē) refers to the Gentiles as distinct from the Jews (Rom 15:11-12; Eph 2:11).

Both Jewish and Christian apocalyptic writings spoke of two judgments at the end of time, the judgment of Israel and the judgment of the Gentiles. Paul follows this common understanding of the Last Judgment when he speaks of Israel being judged first and then the Gentiles (Rom 2:1-11). As salvation came first to the Jews, then to the Gentiles (Rom 1:16), so will come judgment.

In His eschatological teaching at the end of Matthew's gospel, Jesus seems to be following this same distinction. He first tells the parable of the Ten Virgins and the parable of the Talents. These parables of judgment Jesus directs to those who believe in Him as their Lord and Master. Then, in the parable of the Sheep and the Goats, Jesus describes the judgment of non-believers, those who do not know Him and do not believe in Him. That is why He speaks only of charity and kindness as the standard of their judgment.

Thus, with the parable of the Sheep and the Goats, Jesus is holding out the hope of salvation to all people. Even those who never come to know Jesus and believe in Him in this world can be saved. He is excluding no one from the opportunity to merit a place in heaven. Jesus died for all people.

Everyone has the same ultimate vocation. We are all created for union with God in heaven. We come to that union through Jesus Christ, the one mediator and savior of all (1 Tim 2:5; Heb 7:24-25). Those who have no explic-

The Parable of the Sheep and Goats

it faith in Jesus are, through their charity to others, united with Him in his perfect act of charity on the Cross and thus can be saved (*Gaudium et Spes*, 22).

Jesus sat on the Mount of Olives as He spoke about the Last Judgment. In ancient times, this was the posture of authority. He sat when He gave the Sermon on the Mount. According to the parable of the Sheep and Goats, He will sit on His throne of judgment on the last day. The last book of Sacred Scripture takes up this same image of the Lord seated in judgment.

> Then I saw a great white throne, and the one who was seated upon it. The earth and the sky fled so far from his presence that they could no longer be found.
>
> And I saw the dead, great and small, standing before the throne, and the scrolls were opened. Then another scroll was opened, the book of life, and the dead were judged according to their deeds, as were recorded in the scrolls...Anyone who was not found written in the book of life was thrown into the fiery lake. *Rev 20:11-15*

On the last day, Jesus will sit and we will stand before Him. He will judge all people. He will hold those of us who believe in Him accountable for our fidelity to His commandment to love God and one another (Mt 22:37-39; Jn 13:34-35) and to His commission to make disciples of others (Mt 28:19-20). Every thought, word, and deed will be measured against this double standard.

To those on His right, He will say, "Come, you who are blessed by my Father. Inherit the kingdom prepared for you from the foundation of the world." God has prepared heaven to be our true home. "We have here no lasting city" (Heb 13:14).

From the very foundation of the world, that is, from all eternity, God created the world and put us in it so that we could go to heaven after our earthly pilgrimage. The letter to the Ephesians opens with the following doxology of exuberant praise, extolling this purpose of God creating and redeeming us in Christ.

> Blessed be the God,
> and Father of our Lord Jesus Christ,
> who has blessed us in Christ
> with every spiritual blessing in the heavens.
> Before the foundation of the world
> he chose us in Christ
> to be holy and blameless in his sight
> and to be filled with love.
> He predestined us
> for adoption as his children
> through Jesus Christ,
> in accordance with his purpose and pleasure,
> to the praise of the glory
> of his grace
> that he so freely bestowed on us
> in the Beloved. *Eph 1:3-6*

We are made for heaven. Every one of us! No exceptions. For this reason, the first letter to Timothy urges us to pray for all in authority, especially non-Christians.

> To do so is right and acceptable to God our Savior,
> who desires everyone to be saved and to come to
> full knowledge of the truth.
>
> For there is one God,
> and there is one mediator between God and man,
> Christ Jesus, himself a man,
> who gave himself as a ransom for all. *1 Tim 2:3-6*

The Parable of the Sheep and Goats

God wants all to be saved. And so should we! His heart will overflow with joy on the last day when He invites those on His right to enter heaven.

To those on His left, Jesus will say, "Depart from me, you accursed, into the eternal fire prepared for the devil and his angels." Hell was made not for us, but for the devil and the fallen angels. Hell is not a very popular idea in a culture that denies the very concept of sin and canonizes everyone at their death. For many, hell smacks of the outdated idea of the wrath of God.

Reinhold Niebuhr, a Reformed theologian once dubbed "America's theologian," summed up this way of thinking by saying, "A God without wrath bringing men without sin into a kingdom without judgment through the ministrations of a Christ without a Cross." But, there is no Christianity without the Cross. The Cross is the triumph of love over hatred, grace over sin, goodness over indifference. The Cross is Christ's victory over the powers of hell.

To deny hell is to deny the redemption wrought by Christ and to demean the value of human acts. "To disbelieve in hell is to assert that the consequences of good and bad acts are indifferent...Have you ever noticed saints fear hell but never deny it, and great sinners deny hell, but they do not fear it — for the moment. The devil is never so strong as when he gets a man to deny there is a devil" (Venerable Fulton Sheen).

Think about this for a moment. With the parable of the Sheep and the Goats, He whom John the Baptist identified as the Lamb of God who takes away the sins of the world claims to be the Judge of all people on the last day. What a shocking statement! He is now seated on His throne of mercy. Then He will be seated on His throne of judgment. The eternal destiny of every person who ever lived will be determined on each person's relationship to Him. What an unprecedented claim!

Throughout His entire ministry, Jesus silenced those who announced Him as Messiah. Now, hours before the Cross, He proclaims Himself the divine Judge of the world and King of all creation. Only a fool would ignore this claim and dismiss His teachings.

C. S. Lewis once wrote: "Either this man was, and is, the Son of God, or else a madman or something worse. You can shut him up for a fool, you can spit at him and kill him as a demon or you can fall at his feet and call him Lord and God, but let us not come with any patronizing nonsense about his being a great human teacher. He has not left that open to us. He did not intend to...Now it seems to me obvious that He was neither a lunatic nor a fiend: and consequently, however strange or terrifying or unlikely it may seem, I have to accept the view that He was and is God" (C.S. Lewis, *Mere Christianity*, p. 32).

As Judge of the world, Jesus holds out to us two eternal alternatives. Heaven and hell. It is not for us to accept the one and deny the other. How different our lives would be if we took Jesus' words about hell seriously. Heaven would begin even now!

CHAPTER 7

The Parable of the Tower of Siloam

On the Feast of All Saints, November 1, 1755, an earthquake hit the city of Lisbon, Portugal. Less than an hour later, a tsunami engulfed the harbor and downtown area, rushing up the Tagus River. Eighty-five percent of Lisbon's buildings were destroyed. According to some estimates, almost 100,000 residents of Lisbon and surrounding towns lost their lives. Shocks from the earthquake were felt throughout Europe, even as far away as the Caribbean.

Throughout history, disasters have happened again and again. Somewhere around 1500 B.C., a volcanic eruption and an ensuing tsunami completely wiped out the Minoan civilization on the Mediterranean island of Stroggli (known today as Santorini). An earthquake and the fires it caused destroyed Antioch in 526 A.D., taking the lives of thousands who were celebrating the feast of the Ascension. The 1138 Aleppo earthquake killed almost 200,000 people in Syria. The 1871 Peshtigo fire claimed the lives of 2,500 Wisconsin residents. The 1907 Chinese famine took the lives of twenty million people. Hurricane Katrina devastated the gulf coast of the United States in 2005. And, the Covid 19 pandemic worked its havoc on the lives of millions of people around the world. Just to name a few disasters!

Earthquakes, tsunamis, pandemics, floods, and fires leave us questioning. Are these disasters coming from the hand of God? These recurring scenes of immense human suffering, of pain and death make us wonder whether or not these tragic events are the wrath of God Himself.

Great minds have wrestled with this problem. Theologians like Paul, Augustine, and Origen. Philosophers such as Voltaire, Rousseau, and Descartes. Writers such as Dostoevsky, Camus, and C. S. Lewis. Filmmakers such as Bergman and Hitchcock. No age goes without scrutinizing its understanding of God and His providence. No surprise, therefore, that the question why evil happens was placed before Jesus in His public ministry.

Jesus was on His way to Jerusalem when certain Jews approached Him. They reported to Jesus a recent massacre of His fellow Galileans by Pilate. In responding to them, Jesus compares that bloodbath with the collapse of the tower of Siloam killing eighteen people. Thus, He widens the discussion about evil perpetrated by man to include a natural disaster which, in the eyes of His listeners, was done by God.

> At that time some people who were present told Jesus about the Galileans whose blood Pilate had mingled with the blood of their sacrifices. He asked them, "Do you think that because these Galileans suffered in this way they were worse sinners than all other Galileans? No, I tell you. But unless you repent, you will all perish as they did. Or those eighteen people who were killed when the tower at Siloam fell on them—do you think they were more guilty from all the others who were living in Jerusalem? No, I tell you—but unless you repent, you will all perish as they did." *Lk 13:1-5*

The Jews specifically bring to Jesus for comment this fresh massacre of Galileans in the Temple, because Jesus Himself was a Galilean. In one sense, they were appealing to Jesus' sympathy for His fellow countrymen. But there is more to their inquiry.

The Parable of the Tower of Siloam

The Jews' question about the Galileans whose blood Pilate had mingled with the blood of their sacrifices is freighted with political overtones. Tensions between the Jews and the Romans were high. Pilate's administration was turbulent, marked by uprisings and bloodshed. At the least provocation, he was poised to exert his authority.

The Jewish historian Flavius Josephus tells us that once 3,000 Jews were slaughtered at the very moment that the Passover sacrifices were being offered in the Temple. Their corpses were left defiling the Temple courts (Ant.17:9.3; 20:5.3). On another occasion, Pilate dispatched disguised legionaries armed with daggers into the Passover crowds (Ant.18:31). He was jealous of maintaining order and knew that Jewish law forbade the Jews to go armed on the Passover.

Just as they did with the question of whether or not it is lawful to pay tax to Caesar (Lk 20:22), the Jews are setting a trap for Jesus. If Jesus condemns Pilate, they can easily hand Him over to Pilate and thus cut short His ministry and life. If Jesus does not condemn Pilate, He loses the masses who were looking to Him as their long-awaited Messiah, the one who would overthrow their Roman oppressors.

Faced with their ploy to ensnare Him, Jesus reminds them of the recent collapse of the tower of Siloam. A tower built for safety had suddenly become the instrument of death. The tower most likely was part of the public works which Pilate was undertaking in his construction of a new aqueduct. To finance this project, Pilate had taken money from the Temple treasury and incited the anger of the pious Jews.

Money in the sacred treasury was *Corban*, that is, given as a gift to God (Mk 7:11). It could be used solely for religious purposes. In the popular mentality, the recent collapse of the tower of Siloam and the death of eighteen men was an act of God's judgment on Pilate's sacrilege. It was fresh in the minds of those questioning Jesus. And so Jesus introduces this disaster into the discussion. He does not get entangled in their political trap, but forces them to widen their perspective on the question of evil.

In true rabbinic fashion, Jesus questions those questioning Him. Do you think that because these Galileans suffered in this way they were greater sinners than all other Galileans? By no means!...Or those eighteen people who were killed when the tower at Siloam fell on them—do you think they were more guilty than everyone else who lived in Jerusalem? By no means! (Lk 13:2-5).

By comparing an act of man with an act of God, Jesus catches His listeners by surprise. Many of those listening to Jesus saw the misfortunes of others as a punishment for sin. In the Old Testament, this is exactly how Job's friends saw His suffering (Job 4—25). Job's three friends, Eliphaz, Bildad, and Zophar, told Job that his sins had brought about all the calamities that were happening to him. They made the false calculation that sin equals punishment in this world. But, in the Book of Job, God himself rejects their reckoning. "The Lord said to Eliphaz the Temanite, 'My anger blazes against you and your two friends for you have not spoken about me as you should...'" (Job 42:7).

Similarly, Jesus does not equate suffering in this world with a punishment for sin. Once, during the week-long celebration of the Jewish feast of Tabernacles, Jesus left the Temple where He had been teaching and met a man born blind. "His disciples asked him, 'Rabbi, who sinned, this man or his parents, that he was born blind?' Jesus

The Parable of the Tower of Siloam

answered, 'Neither this man nor his parents sinned'" (Jn 9:1-3). If all suffering were God's punishment for sin, there certainly would be much more suffering in the world!

Gifted with reason, we are wired to make judgments. To discern the good from the bad and right from wrong: this is an essential part of our being human. However, every judgment must be founded on truth, not on rumor or on appearance. And it must always be tempered with compassion.

Thus, when told of the slaughter of his fellow Galileans, Jesus refuses to connect suffering with a particular act of sin. A sudden, violent death is not proof of a punishment from God. In effect, Jesus sweeps away all facile theories about God's inscrutable providence.

We cannot deny that there are clear examples of the connection between evil behavior and suffering. Those who do not take proper care of their bodies suffer ill health. Overindulgence in food or alcohol harms the body. Not exercising properly leaves the muscles weak. The reckless, irresponsible destruction of natural resources devastates ecosystems. As the proverb says, "God always forgives, man sometimes forgives, but nature never forgives."

Nonetheless, not every sickness nor every disaster comes from an individual acting irresponsibly. Someone suffering with cancer is no more a sinner than a person in good health. Someone perishing in a car accident is not necessarily a greater sinner than anyone else on the road that day. Someone's house burning to the ground does not mean its owner is guiltier of more sin than his neighbor. As Jesus says, those butchered in the Temple by Pilate and those crushed to death under the tower of Siloam were not greater sinners than others.

The all-merciful God is all-just. And justice requires that wrongs be righted and evil be punished. But, in this world, the sinner and the saint are equally exposed to calamities and disasters. The good and the bad at times suffer equally. When the kingdom of God comes in its fullness at the end of time, then the wheat and weeds will be separated and everyone will receive their just reward (Mt 13: 24-30, 36-43).

Before the final righting of all wrongs at the end of time, Jesus tells His listeners, they themselves must repent. They are stunned when He says to them, "I tell you, if you do not repent, you will all perish as they did!" He repeats this call to repent a second time. His listeners were not expecting Him to include them among sinners in need of repentance. They wanted Jesus to judge the Romans as sinners, not them.

What courage Jesus has in calling His listeners to repent! On the occasion of His first sermon in the synagogue of Nazareth, Jesus had refused to condone the fierce nationalism of His day which divided the righteous Jews from the unrighteous Gentiles. As a result, "all the people in the synagogue were roused with fury. They leapt up, drove him out of the town, and led him to the top of the hill upon which their town was built, intending to hurl him off the cliff" (Lk 4:28-29). Now in the Temple in Jerusalem, Jesus once again challenges the Jews with their need to repent; and, they become angry and all the more intent on killing Him.

Jesus' call to repentance was at the very heart of His message to all. In fact, Jesus begins His public ministry preaching repentance. Like John the Baptist, "Jesus began to preach and say, 'Repent, for the kingdom of heaven is close at hand'" (Mt 4:17). On the lips of John, the ancient

The Parable of the Tower of Siloam

prophets' call for conversion sounded with unusual clarity. John demanded the sinners to throw off their habits of sin, to bring forth righteous acts and to turn their hearts back to God. John demanded such conversion from all, the public sinner and the outwardly pious.

Jesus repeats the same imperative, "Repent." But it is new. It is fresh. It is Spirit-filled. Unlike John, Jesus does not call for repentance as a preparation for the kingdom. No! Repentance is the effect of the kingdom already present. God is bringing about the kingdom in the ministry of His Son. We can turn to God with our whole life because God is turning to us in Jesus. This is good news. God's grace grounds the possibility for our believing and turning from sin.

During His very brief public ministry, Jesus continually reaches out to sinners. He shows how our repentance is a response to God's grace. At the very beginning of His ministry, Jesus meets Matthew seated in the customs house in Capernaum. This tax-collector is despised by his countrymen. Yet Jesus calls him from the tax-collector's table to table-fellowship with Himself. In that personal exchange of friendship offered and received, Matthew comes to forgiveness. First comes the gift of God's love in Jesus. Then comes repentance. From the employ of the Roman emperor, Matthew enters the service of genuine royalty. He follows Jesus with his life (Mk 2:13-17).

At the very end of His public ministry, Jesus encounters another tax-collector. Jesus is passing through the oasis town of Jericho. He is on the Roman road at the point where it begins its ascent from the Judean desert up to Jerusalem. He is just sixteen miles away from His appointed destiny in the Holy City. The crowd presses in on Him.

The curious Zacchaeus scurries up a sycamore tree to catch a glimpse of Jesus. Jesus looks up at Zacchaeus, singles him out and invites Himself to his house.

Zacchaeus opens the door of his home to Jesus. And, in that offer of hospitality, Jesus welcomes him into the kingdom. Overjoyed with the gift of salvation, the tax-collector repents of his past. Now a believer, he no longer takes from others, but freely gives even beyond what the law required (Lk 19:1-10). The gift of Jesus' friendship first. Then repentance.

By using the tower of Siloam as a parable, Jesus is teaching us that natural calamities just as personal misfortunes continually plague our world. Even if we escape them, not one of us is exempt from the sad sentence of death which we inherit from Adam and Eve. "All have sinned and are deprived of the glory of God" (Rom 3:23). By our sins, we are destined to perish.

Jesus says, "No, I tell you, but unless you repent, you will all perish (ἀπολεῖσθε: apoleisthe) as they did" (Lk 13:3, 5). This Greek word for perish is used throughout the New Testament to mean eternal punishment. With this word, Jesus moves His discussion with the Jews away from their philosophical questioning about divine providence. He does not satisfy their desire to know why good people suffer bad things. But Jesus sweeps aside all idle speculation and gets to the most important issue we all must face: what will be our eternal destiny.

Jesus is calling us to repent, just as He called the people of His day. "The time has come...Repent and believe the Good News" (Mk 1:15). He addresses us with the present imperative because our turning from sin and turning to God, our repentance and our faith, are a continuous process throughout our life. Repentance is letting God take control of our lives so that He may lead us to Himself.

CHAPTER 8

The Parable of the Barren Fig Tree

For millennia before the invention of writing, people passed on their stories, their histories and their culture by means of an oral tradition. The Mesopotamian *Epic of Gilgamesh* and the medieval English *Beowulf* were passed on by word of mouth for centuries before being committed to a text.

In *Phaedrus*, his 4th century work on the art of rhetoric, Plato, records Socrates' discussion of the Egyptian myth about the invention of writing. Socrates has the Egyptian god Ammon mouth Socrates' own view about writing. Ammon says, "This discovery of yours will create forgetfulness in the learners' souls, because they will not use their memories; they will trust to the external written characters and not remember themselves." Socrates, the founder of Western philosophy, feared that writing would diminish the essential role that memorization played in preserving the wisdom of the past.

At the time of Jesus, education was based on memorization. Rabbi Akiva was one of Judaism's most famous and revered teachers. He described first century Jewish education by saying: "The teacher should strive to make the lesson agreeable to the pupils by clear reasons, as well as frequent repetitions, until they thoroughly understand the matter, and are able to recite it with great fluency."

Jesus certainly knew that, if His teachings were to be passed on to others, His disciples needed to memorize them. Therefore, as a wise and compassionate teacher, Jesus taught in such a way that they could remember what He said. For example, as we read the Beatitudes in Matthew's gospel, we can easily discern in the two sets of four beatitudes a repetitive pattern that facilitates memorization (Mt 5:3-10).

Poetry, with its recurring patterns, fixed structure, figurative language, alliteration, and assonance, facilitates memorization. No wonder Jesus framed nearly eighty percent of His teachings in poetic form. Many of Jesus' sayings follow the basic style of Hebrew poetry. Simply stated, Hebrew poetry consists in saying one thing and then repeating it a second time in such a way that both sentences parallel one another.

Thus, when Jesus gives us the *Our Father*, He says, "Lead us not into temptation, but deliver us from evil." Both parallel phrases express in different words the same petition to be kept from evil (Mt 6:14). Likewise, when Jesus teaches His disciples about giving good example, He first speaks about salt enhancing the flavor of food and then repeats the same idea with the image of a light on a lampstand illuminating a house (Mt 5:13-15).

To an extraordinary degree, Jesus uses in His teaching mnemonic devices such as synonymous and antithetical parallelism, alliteration, and play on words. He skillfully planned His lessons in such a way that His words would strike the ear of His followers and remain wedged in their memory. He wanted all His listeners to remember what He said; and, He intended His disciples to carry His teaching far beyond the confines of first century Judea. What great love Jesus had for His disciples to spend much time preparing His teachings so well!

In His last appearance in the gospel of Matthew, the Risen Lord says, "Go, therefore, and make disciples of all nations, baptizing them in the name of the Father, and of the Son, and of the Holy Spirit, and teaching them to observe all that I have commanded you. And behold,

The Parable of the Barren Fig Tree

I am with you always, until the end of the world" (Mt 28:19-20). But, long before this last instruction, Jesus had prepared His students to be good teachers for the next generation of believers. He left them with no book in their hands, but with His message etched in their memory.

As a good teacher, Jesus liked to express His teaching with an apt illustration and then reinforce His thought by giving a second example similar to the first. For instance, He says, "No one sews a patch of unshrunken cloth on an old cloak, because the patch eventually pulls away from the cloak, and a worse tear results. Nor do people pour new wine into old wineskins for if they do, the wineskins burst; the wine spills forth, and the skins are ruined. Rather, they pour new wine into fresh wineskins. In this way both are preserved" (Mt 9:16-17).

In these brief illustrations, Jesus is teaching that the kingdom of God that He proclaims is a new reality. It cannot be simply accommodated and adjusted to fit what has gone before. The economy of salvation inaugurated with Jesus demands new ways of acting and new forms of expression. Jesus repeats the same thought with two different images. This repetition aids memorization.

Jesus seems to have been fond of telling two similar parables, one following the other. Thus, He recounts the parable of the Lost Sheep and then the parable of the Lost Coin (Lk 15:4-10); the Hidden Treasure followed by the Pearl of Great Price (Mt 13:44-46); the Tower Builder followed by the Warring King (Lk 14:28-33); and, the Mustard Seed and then the Leaven (Lk 13:18-21). With an economy of words, these twin parables told together were easily remembered.

The parable of the Barren Fig Tree which we are now examining is twin to the parable of the Tower of Siloam.

With the parable of the Tower, Jesus calls His Jewish listeners to repent. Then, with the parable of the Barren Fig Tree, He warns them of the consequences of not repenting. Both parables reveal something of the mystery of God who is all-just and all-merciful.

> Then he told them this parable: "A man had a fig tree planted in his vineyard, but whenever he came looking for fruit on it, he found none. Therefore, he said to his vinedresser, 'For three years I have come looking for fruit on this fig tree and have never found any. Cut it down! Why should it continue to use up the soil?' But the vinedresser replied, 'Sir, let it alone for one more year while I dig around it and fertilize it. Perhaps it will bear fruit next year. If so, well and good. If not, then you can cut it down.' "
>
> *Lk 13:6-9*

This parable is found only in Luke. However, it closely resembles the incident of Jesus' cursing a fig tree during the last Passover of His life. After His Palm Sunday entrance into Jerusalem, Jesus spends the night in Bethany. On Monday morning, He returns to the city. On His way into Jerusalem, He spots a barren fig tree.

> On the next day, as they were leaving Bethany, he felt hungry. Noticing in the distance a fig tree in leaf, he went to see if he could find any fruit on it. When he reached it, he found nothing except leaves, since it was not the season for figs. Then he said to it, "May no one ever again eat fruit from your branches." And his disciples heard him say this.
>
> *Mk 11:12-14*

After cursing the barren tree, Jesus goes to the Temple. Pious pilgrims flooded the city from all over the Roman world. With a bit of exaggeration, the Jewish historian

The Parable of the Barren Fig Tree

Flavius Josephus numbers the city's Passover population at 250,000. He wishes to impress his readers with the throngs crowding the Holy City.

As Jesus enters Jerusalem, the air is thick with religiosity. The smell of incense wafting in the breeze. The smoke of sacrifice rising to the heavens. The shouts of hawkers peddling their goods. The trumpet blasts summoning to prayer. It is the gladdest time of the year.

Pilgrims have come to offer their sacrifices. It was the duty of the priests to examine whether or not their animals were fit for sacrifice. Any animal presented to the Lord had to be without a blemish or imperfection. Not surprisingly, quite often when a pilgrim presented his own animal, the priests declared the animal unfit. As a result, the pilgrim was forced to buy an approved animal kept in the courtyards of the Temple.

For those who came from afar, the sheer inconvenience of bringing an animal from home made it easier for them to buy the approved animals from the merchants in the Temple area. The prices of these animals were highly inflated. For example, a dove that cost fifteen cents was sold for fifteen dollars. In addition, the pilgrims had to exchange their own currency into Temple currency to buy the animals. They paid heavily for the transaction. All this extortion of pilgrims who wished to honor God stirred Jesus to righteous anger.

When Jesus enters the Temple courts, He sees the merchants and money changers in the Temple courts. Those profiting from the piety of others were perverting religion. With whip in hand, He overthrows their tables, driving them from the Temple. The Jewish leaders become alarmed.

On the previous day, Jesus had allowed the crowds to openly hail Him as the Messiah. He never permitted that before. His action of cleansing the Temple now raises the people's Messianic expectations to a fever pitch. For the prophet Malachi had predicted that, when the Messiah finally came, he would cleanse the Temple. He said, "And suddenly the Lord whom you seek will come to his temple,... He will sit refining and purifying; he will purify the descendants of Levi..." (Mal 3:1, 3).

The leaders fear an uprising. They want to avoid bloodshed at the hands of the Romans ever ready to squelch any uprising incited by a would-be Messiah. And so to protect their own interests, the chief priests and scribes plot to kill Jesus (Mk 11:18). All the while, when they are conspiring against Him, Jesus continues to teach in the Temple. At the end of the day, Jesus leaves Jerusalem and spends the night outside the city. He returns to the Temple the next day.

Early the next morning, as they passed by, they saw the fig tree withered away to its roots. Then Peter recalling and said to him, "Rabbi, look! The fig tree that you cursed has withered." Jesus said to them,"Have faith in God. Amen, I say to you, whoever says to this mountain, 'Be lifted up and thrown into the sea,' and does not doubt in his heart but believes that what he says will happen, it will be accomplished for him." *Mk 11:20-23; Mt 21:18-22*

It is shocking for us to see Jesus curse a tree, making it wither from its roots, never to produce a single fig. Jesus appears unreasonably angry. Why should a barren fig tree suffer such wrath?

Never once in the entire gospel tradition does Jesus ever work a miracle of power for His own benefit or as a punishment for someone. All Jesus' actions are merciful and selfless. This incident is totally out of character with every other work of Jesus.

The Parable of the Barren Fig Tree

Some scholars hold that, on His way into Jerusalem, Jesus saw a barren fig tree, pointed to it, saying that it would never have time to produce fruit before He accomplishes the great events of our salvation. Over the course of time, Jesus' saying became the story of the cursed fig tree. Such an explanation is hardly satisfying. It attributes too much creative liberty to the oral tradition before the gospels were written.

Other scholars, however, say that gentle Luke received from tradition the event of Jesus' cursing the fig tree and was dismayed by it. So he transformed it into a parable in order not to cast Jesus in a negative light. This explanation is also not satisfying.

Luke himself tells Theophilus, the recipient of his gospel, that he was very careful in doing his research before writing his gospel.

> Since many different individuals have undertaken the task to set down an account of the events that have been fulfilled among us, in accordance with their transmission to us by those who were eyewitnesses and ministers of the word from the beginning, I too after researching all the evidence anew with great care, have decided to write an orderly account for you, Theophilus, who are so greatly revered... *Lk 1:1-3*

It is most unlikely that Luke would deliberately change an event into a parable! In Mark's gospel, the narrative of the cursed fig tree climaxes with its destruction. But this element of destruction is totally lacking in Luke's parable. The parable receives its meaning from the very fact that the barren fig tree is not destroyed.

Simply put, Mark and Luke relate two separate incidents in the life of Jesus. On one occasion, Jesus tells a parable. On another, He curses a fig tree. But this still leaves us very uneasy. We can readily accept a parable about a barren tree. But how can we accept Jesus destroying a poor fig tree with a curse? Let us look at this recorded event more carefully, trying to appreciate the culture in which Jesus lived.

Fig trees produce figs before putting forth their leaves. When Jesus sees the fig tree on His way into Jerusalem, it captures His attention. This tree is proudly flaunting its leaves, beckoning the passerby to come and taste of its fruit. But there are no figs. It is falsely advertising its fruitfulness.

Jesus has witnessed enough of the false piety of those who display their public acts to be seen. He sees the pretense of holiness in the Temple. Sweet music. Elaborate liturgies without the fruit of charity. The racketeering. The extortion of the poor. As Adam tried to cover his nakedness with fig leaves, too many worshipers, especially the leaders, were attempting to conceal their spiritual nakedness with their outward show.

Jesus is angry, not because there is no religious activity, but because it is false. Like Elijah who cursed the House of Ahab and like Elisha who cursed the unruly children who mocked him, Jesus utters a curse. Blessings and curses came from His sacred lips as from those of the prophets of old (Lk 6:20-26). Jesus stands in the noble tradition of Old Testament prophets such as Ahijah, Isaiah, Jeremiah, and Ezekiel. And, like them, He uses a symbolic act to visualize His prophecy.

The withered fig tree, forlorn and barren, is the symbol of imminent destruction awaiting an unrepentant Jerusalem. The real miracle is that Jesus' curse falls on a tree and not on the people who anger Him. He is truly

The Parable of the Barren Fig Tree

the compassionate Savior who gives a somber warning to Jerusalem and to us that only repentance can save us from ultimate doom.

We can now turn our attention from the cursing of the fig tree to the parable of the Barren Fig Tree. In the parable, Jesus speaks of a vineyard. His description of the vineyard parallels the picture which He depicts in the parable of the Tenants ((Mt 21:33-46; Mk 12:1-12; Lk 20:9-19). In the figurative language of Scripture, the vineyard is a well-known symbol.

The prophet Isaiah uses the vineyard as the symbol of the entire Jewish nation. He says, "The vineyard of the Lord of hosts is the house of Israel, and the people of Judah are the plant he cherished" (Isa 5:7). The psalmist likewise uses the same image for the nation. "You brought a vine out of Egypt; you dispersed the nations and planted it. You prepared the ground for it; then it took root and filled the land" (Ps 80:9-10). Thus, on Jesus' lips, the vineyard is the whole Jewish people.

But, what about the fig tree in the vineyard? It is no ordinary tree. It is fruitful above other trees. When mature, it can bear fruit in spring, in summer, in autumn, and sometimes even in winter. It is a tree of noble character planted in a vineyard which symbolizes the whole nation.

In the parable of the Tower, Jesus addresses the crowds. In this parable that follows immediately, He narrows His audience to a group of people within the whole nation. He addresses the leaders. They had many privileges. They occupied a choice spot in the Lord's vineyard. With their honor came responsibility. They who were expected to give abundant examples of faith and charity. But they did not!

The parable vividly reflects the gardening practices of Jesus' day. Landowners would select a fertile spot on their property to plant their vineyard. They would cultivate it, eager for its grapes and their sweet juice. Not to waste precious soil, they would plant fig trees in the corners of the vineyard. Both vines and fig trees were highly valued.

The landowner would leave the work of cultivating his fig trees to his gardener. This was a tedious task, requiring years of work and much patience. For the first three years, the young fig tree produced no fruit. For the next three years, its figs were small and without taste. The gardener would remove them to allow the tree to become stronger, eventually producing a rich and abundant harvest.

According to Levitical law (Lev 19:23-25), the fruit could not be eaten for another three years. It was considered unclean, that is, not yet sanctified by the offering of the first fruits to God. Thus, the owner waited patiently for six years. In the seventh year, the owner would dedicate the fruit of his tree to God before using the tree for himself. God came first! Nothing but the best for God! A lesson for us.

To dedicate the produce of his tree to God, the owner would go to Jerusalem either to share his produce with the poor or to spend a fifth part of its value to feed the poor. God was honored and given due praise by feeding the hungry. "He who oppresses the poor insults their Creator, but the one who is kind to the needy does him honor" (Prov 14:31).

Thus, when we give to the poor, we should give not grudgingly as a duty discharged, but cheerfully as a joyful thanksgiving to God for all that He gives us. As St. Paul admonishes us, "Each person should give as much as he

The Parable of the Barren Fig Tree

has decided in his heart, not with reluctance or under compulsion, for God loves a cheerful giver" (2 Cor 9:7).

When the owner in Jesus' parable finally comes looking for figs to eat for himself and finds none, he becomes angry and impatient. He tells the gardener, "I have come in search of fruit on this fig tree but have found none." The long time of waiting has passed. No fruit. The situation is hopeless. The owner barks the order to his gardener to cut it down.

The landowner does not want the barren fig tree to deplete the richness of the soil. Not only is the tree useless; it has become harmful to the vineyard itself. It prevents the other plants from growing. He could plant a productive tree in its place. In the owner's judgment, the vineyard is better off without the sterile fig tree.

Many listening to Jesus' parable had heard John the Baptist preach, using the very same image of a barren tree. The crowds flocked to him and John thundered at them an ominous summons to repentance. He threatened them with punishment if they did not repent.

> He admonished the crowds who came out to be baptized by him, "You brood of vipers! Who warned you to flee from the wrath to come? Produce good fruits as proof of your repentane. Do not begin to say to yourselves, 'We have Abraham as our father,' for I tell you, God is able to raise up children to Abraham from these stones. Even now the ax is laid to the root of the trees. Therefore, every tree that does not bear good fruit will be cut down and thrown into the fire." *Lk 3:7-9*

In Jesus' parable, the landowner says exactly what Jesus' listeners were expecting him to say, namely "Cut it down!" This is what happens to the unfruitful vine in Isaiah's parable of the vineyard. The wall protecting it is broken down. The land is made waste. The vine destroyed. No more time to spare after judgment has been pronounced. No more effort. Judgment and then punishment.

But Jesus surprises His audience with the response of the gardener. He intervenes and pleas for patience. "Sir, leave it for this year also, and I shall cultivate the ground around it and fertilize it; it may bear fruit in the future. If not, you can cut it down." One more year. Let us wait and see! No immediate justice, but mercy! Is not this characteristic of the entire ministry of Jesus?

Jesus also catches His audience off guard with a bit of humor that brings a smile to their lips. The gardener says that he will spread fertilizer around the roots of the tree. The Greek word κόπρια (kopria) in the text actually means manure or dung. If the tree symbolizes the religious leaders and not just the people, the unpleasant image of smelly dung spread over them would have delighted the ordinary person.

Jesus ends the parable abruptly. He leaves us questioning whether or not the extra care and time have an effect. He deliberately provides no answer, because we must answer the question with our lives. Throughout His whole ministry, He preached the need to repent and bring forth the fruits of faith and charity. He waited for the response of His listeners. He waits for ours.

Ultimately, Jesus' parable of the Barren Fig Tree is not simply a warning to change the way we live. It is His challenge to change the way we think about God. It is a parable that makes us face both the justice and the mercy of God. So often we do not produce the fruits of righteousness, "love, joy, peace, patience, kindness, generosity, faithfulness, gentleness, self-control" (Gal 5: 22-23). Yet, God is patient.

God told Adam, "You can eat of any of the trees in the garden, but you must never eat from the tree of the knowledge of good and evil. If you were to eat from it, you would surely die" (Gen 2:17). Adam and Eve ate of the forbidden fruit, but did not die immediately. Jonah went to Nineveh and prophesied as the Lord commanded him, "Forty days more and Nineveh shall be overthrown" (Jon 3:3). But Nineveh repented and was not destroyed in forty days. In God, both justice and mercy are one. That is why God proclaims His name to Moses in the Exodus events saying, "The Lord, the Lord, a compassionate and gracious God, slow to anger and abounding in steadfast love and fidelity" (Ex 34:6).

God's forbearance is meant to lead us to repentance (Rom 2:4). His patience is revealed to us in the meek and gentle Christ. "The Lord ...is patient with you. It is not his wish that any should perish but rather that all should be brought to repentance" (2 Pet 3:9). The sun shines abundantly on a dung heap, but the filth remains unchanged. But God's patient love shines on the repentant soul and transforms it as gold shining in the noonday sun.

In Jesus' parable of the Wicked Tenants (Mt 21:33-41), the owner of the vineyard who brings the wicked tenants to a bad end is clearly God. So also in the parable of the Barren Fig Tree, the landowner who orders the tree to be cut down represents God who passes a just judgment on our sins. But the gardener who intervenes and pleads for more time represents Christ Himself, our advocate before the throne of God.

At the Last Supper, Jesus already knows that the disciples will lose faith at His crucifixion. They will abandon

Him. He tells Peter, "Simon, Simon, behold Satan has desired to sift all of you like wheat, but I have prayed that your own faith may not fail. And once you have turned back, you must strengthen your brethren" (Lk 22:31-32). He intercedes for Peter and all His disciples. In saying to them, "I will ask the Father, and he will give you another Advocate to be with you forever, the Spirit of truth..." (Jn 14:16-17), Jesus is telling them that He, too, is their Advocate before the Father.

When we look at our many sins, we can well fear the awesome holiness of God and cry out in the words of Isaiah the prophet "Woe is me! I am doomed. For I am a man of unclean lips, and I live among a people of unclean lips" (Isa 6:5). But, when we turn our gaze to Christ in heaven, we see our great high priest who gave His life for us. He is pleading our case not on our merits but with the atonement He made for us on Golgotha. "He has the full power to save those who approach God through him, since he lives forever to intercede for them" (Heb 7:25). In the court of heaven, He is winning our case, while on earth He is working in us to bring forth the precious fruit of righteousness.

CHAPTER 9

The Parable of the Narrow Door

Isidor I. Rabi won the Nobel laureate in physics for his discovery of nuclear magnetic resonance. It is used in radiology to form pictures of the anatomy. When asked why he became a scientist and not a doctor or lawyer like other immigrant children in his neighborhood, he gave a classic response.

"My mother," he said, "made me a scientist without ever intending it. Every other Jewish mother in Brooklyn would ask her child after school: 'So? Did you learn anything today?' But not my mother. She always asked me a different question. 'Izzy,' she would say, 'did you ask a good question today?' That difference—asking good questions—made me become a scientist!"

A wise mother understood the importance of the right question. And so did other enlightened minds! Socrates, Plato, and Aristotle searched for the right question to lead others to knowledge. Nobel Prize physicist Albert Einstein once said, "If I had an hour to solve a problem and my life depended on the solution, I would spend the first fifty-five minutes determining the proper question to ask... for once I know the proper question, I could solve the problem in less than five minutes."

In the gospels, Jesus frequently asks questions of others. Of two disciples of John the Baptist, "What do you want?" (Jn 1:38). Of the Samaritan woman at the well, "Will you give me a drink?" (Jn 4:7). Of a certain rich official, "Why do you call me good?" (Lk 18:19). Of two blind men, "What do you want me to do for you?" (Mt 20:32).

According to one estimate, Jesus asked as many as 307 questions. That is almost three times more than the 113 questions which He answered. The world's greatest teacher knew how important the right question is. Moreover, in preaching the kingdom of God, Jesus preferred not to get entangled in abstract theological discussions. Rather, He spoke to concrete situations, challenging individuals to enter the kingdom.

Once, as Jesus was on His way to Jerusalem, He "passed through towns and villages, teaching as he made his way... Someone asked him, 'Lord, will only a few be saved?'" (Lk 13:22-23) This was a hotly debated question in that day. Will all of Israel be saved? What about the Gentiles? There was much discussion and speculation. Not all the answers were optimistic.

The Second Book of Esdras, an apocalyptic book written around the time of Jesus, reflects the attitude of those Jews who leaned too heavily on their bloodline from Abraham. Their pride in being part of the Chosen People led them to espouse a harsh exclusiveness. "The Most High has made this world for many, but the world to come for few" (2 Esd 8:1). "There are many more of them which perish than of them which shall be saved... as a wave is greater than a drop" (2 Esd 9:15-16). "Let the multitude perish then" (2 Esd 9:22).

The unnamed man who questions Jesus about the number of the saved grew up in an atmosphere where there was a strong emphasis on the doctrine of election. The Jews were chosen. The Gentiles were not! What was the opinion of the young rabbi from Nazareth on this topic important to so many?

The man questioning Jesus may well have been one of His own followers. He addresses Jesus as "Lord." Seeing the small following Jesus has, is it not possible that He is honestly asking whether only the few who accept Jesus as Messiah would enter the kingdom? Or, perhaps, is he worried because Jesus is welcoming the sinners and outcasts? Will these too be saved? Is he, in a more general way, raising the thorny question of predestination? The gospel text gives us no reason for his question.

The question itself places Jesus on the spot. If Jesus responds by saying that there are indeed few in number to be saved, He would be giving His blessing to the harsh, jealous, exclusive attitude of some of His contemporaries. If Jesus says that there will be many who will be saved, He would be quenching the fierce nationalism of others and would be judged disloyal to His own people.

Masterfully, Jesus moves the discussion away from the general to the specific. He sidesteps the speculative question whether few will be saved. No longer is it a matter of how many will be saved. Rather, He turns the spotlight on the man questioning. Will he be one of the saved or not? He answered, "Strive to enter through the narrow door, for many, I tell you, will try to enter but will not succeed in doing so" (Lk 13:24).

On such an important matter as one's salvation, discussing the issue theoretically pales before the imperative of doing all one can do to be saved. And so Jesus issues a command that applies to this man and to all of us: "Strive to enter by the narrow door."

Jesus' one line answer is actually a short parable. He is using an image familiar to His audience in an attempt to lead them to the truth about the kingdom of God. Jesus speaks of "the narrow door." The Greek word θύρα (thura) can be translated either as "door" or "gate." It is not improbable that Jesus was near some small town on a hill. Pointing to the steep winding road leading to the narrow entrance to the city, He spoke of the effort needed to climb the ascent and make one's way through the narrow opening in the city wall. Ordinary people would immediately understand this image.

To the learned, Jesus' metaphor would have echoed the *Tabula of Cebes*. Although this work is ascribed to the fourth century Pythagorean philosopher Cebes, a disciple of Socrates, it actually comes from around the time of Jesus. The work, a forerunner of John Bunyons' *The Pilgrims' Progress*, depicts human life as a journey beset with the trials and temptations that thwart true happiness. The *Tabula of Cebes* was well known throughout antiquity. Sounding very much like Jesus, Cebes gives this advice: "Seest thou not a certain small door, and a pathway before the door, in no way crowded, but few, very few, go in...? This is the way that leadeth to true disciple" (*Tabula*, c.16).

Jesus' teaching is not unlike the advice of many others over the centuries. For example, the 5th century Greek playwright Aeschylus wrote, "Happiness is a choice that requires effort at times." Franklin Delano Roosevelt similarly quipped, "Happiness lies not in the mere possession of money; it lies in the joy of achievement, in the thrill of creative effort." Helen Keller reminded others that "true happiness...is not attained through self-gratification, but through a fidelity to a worthy purpose." At face value, Jesus' words can be taken as a piece of common wisdom.

When Jesus says, "Strive to enter through the narrow door," He is reminding us that there is no such thing as cheap grace. Dietrich Bonhoeffer, an evangelical pastor and a vocal critic of Nazism, coined this expression "cheap grace." In his 1937 classic work *The Cost of*

Discipleship, Bonhoeffer defined "cheap grace" as "the preaching of forgiveness without requiring repentance, baptism without church discipline, communion without confession. Cheap grace is grace without discipleship, grace without the cross..."

God loves us freely and He desires our response. "God created us without us: but He did not will to save us without us" (St. Augustine, *Sermo* 169, 11.13). Because of our fallen human nature and our past sins, we must make every effort to respond to God's love by living a life worthy of our call (Eph 4:1). The grace Jesus offers us is a gift that we must earnestly desire, seek after, and accept when given to us. It is not cheap. It cost Jesus the Cross. It costs us something. We are not saved by our effort. But we cannot be saved without it. That is why Jesus tells us that we need to make every effort to enter through the narrow door.

Erasmus, one of the greatest scholars of the northern Renaissance, explained why it is difficult for sinners to pass through the narrow door. "In the way, nothing is to be found that flatters the flesh, but many things opposite to it, poverty, fasting, watching, injuries, chastity, and sobriety. And as for the gate, it receives none that are swollen with the glory of this life; none that are elated and lengthened out with pride; none that are distended with luxury; it does not admit those that are laden with the fardels of riches, nor those that drag along with them the other implements of the world. None can pass through it but naked men, who are stripped of all worldly lusts, and who, having, as it were, put off their bodies, are emaciated into spirits, which is the reason that it is sought after by so few."

When Jesus encourages listeners to strive to enter through the narrow door, the New Testament word used for "strive" is the Greek *agónizomai* (agonizomai: literally, to *agonize*). It is an impressive word. It indicates the effort exerted both in mind and body to achieve a goal. It requires the straining of every muscle, the concentrating of one's entire attention, and the exertion of all one's strength.

The Greek word *agónizomai* (agonizomai) that means "to strive" comes from the Greek games. In the Olympics, the wrestlers, boxers, runners, javelin throwers, discus throwers, and charioteers trained long hours for the contest. They strove with all their energy to win so as to be crowned with a wreath of olive leaves. How much more should we be earnest in training ourselves in a virtuous life! "Everyone who seeks a prize submits himself to rigorous discipline in every respect. They do so to win a perishable crown, while we seek an imperishable one" (1 Cor 9:25). Our prize is eternal life.

At the very beginning of His public ministry, Jesus noticed crowds flocking to John the Baptist. Jesus also witnessed the multitudes pressing in on Himself, straining to hear Him and see His works. They were eager for the coming of the kingdom of God in their day. He felt like a city under attack. People were coming at Him from all sides, not even leaving Him time to eat (Mk 3:20). And so He said, "From the days of John the Baptist until now the kingdom of heaven has been subjected to violence, and the violent are taking it by force" (Mt 11:12).

Through Jesus' ministry, the kingdom was being ushered in and only those who were zealously seeking it would enter. St. Ambrose beautifully describes how we should exert ourselves in our following of Christ:

> Whosoever shall do most violence to Christ shall be accounted most religious by Him. We attack Him, not with swords, nor staves, nor stones; but

with meekness, good works, and chastity. These are the weapons of our faith, by which we strive in the contest. But, in order that we may be able to make use of these arms in doing violence, let us first use a certain violence to our own bodies, let us carry by storm the vices of our members, that we may obtain the rewards of valor. For, to seize the Savior's kingdom, we must first reign in ourselves.

Jesus concludes His short parable of striving to enter through the narrow door by saying, "Many, I tell you, will attempt to enter but will not be strong enough." Jesus is not saying that many people will not be saved. Rather, He is affirming that many will not be strong enough on their own. Not even the strongest can achieve salvation on their own.

Actually, entering through the door is possible for all. For Jesus also says,

> Ask, and it will be given to you; seek, and you will find; knock, and the door will be opened to you. For everyone who asks, will receive; and those who seek will find, and to those who knock the door will be opened. *Mt 7:7-8*

God has an open door policy! He shows no favorites. Anyone may be among the number of the saved.

As long as we live in this world, the door to salvation is open. This is the time to seek and to strive. "Behold, now is the acceptable time; behold, now is the day of salvation" (2 Cor 6:2). We must never become so involved in the things of this world that we "neglect so great a salvation" available to us now (Heb 2:3).

In C.S. Lewis' classic *Screwtape Letters*, Satan meets with three of his closest collaborators. Each presents his tactic to populate hell with more people. The last devil offers the best strategy. Just convince people to put off the things of God until tomorrow. Conversion, repentance, and prayer some other time, but not now. Getting people to neglect spiritual matters as things that can be deferred to another day is the fastest and surest way to pack hell.

"Neglect," that is, not paying attention to something in an opportune time, is the slippery road that ends in ruin. A marriage deteriorates when spouses neglect the ordinary courtesies of love. A business goes bankrupt when the owner no longer pays careful attention to his customers. No worldly enterprise achieves success where there is neglect. So also in the weighty matter of our eternal salvation!

On January 30, 1848, 15-year-old Homan Walsh flew his kite from one side of the Niagara Falls Gorge to the other. Someone caught the string at the end of the kite and tied a stronger string. Homan pulled the thicker string back across the gorge. They did this again and again, each time with a stronger string and then finally with a sturdy rope. At last, a steel cable crossed the vast expanse that made possible the building of the bridge over which workers and tourists could pass. It all began with careful attention to a thin string at the end of a kite.

Little things matter, especially in our passing from this side of eternity to the next. "Whoever can be trusted in small matters can also be trusted in great ones.... And if you have not shown yourself to be trustworthy with what belongs to another, who will give you anything of your own?" (Lk 16:10, 12). Great doors turn on small hinges.

Certainly, Jesus' mandate to strive to enter through the narrow door calls us to be serious about our salvation and to make every effort to avoid sin and live virtuously even in the smallest aspect of our lives. But there is much more to His words than a strong moral exhortation. He is making a profound theological statement about God's plan for our salvation.

In John's gospel, Jesus makes seven unique claims about Himself. They all begin with the words "I am." (Jn 6:35; 8:12; 10:9; 10:11; 11:25; 14:16; 15:5). For example, after the multiplication of the loaves and fish, the crowds demand Jesus give them bread just as Moses had given their ancestors manna in the desert. Jesus answers them, saying, "I am the bread of life; whoever comes to me will never hunger, and whoever believes in me will never thirst" (Jn 6:35). Jesus is the unfailing source of life for those who believe in Him.

Once, during the Feast of Tabernacles, Jesus said, "I am the light of the world. The one who follows me will never walk in darkness, rather he will have the light of life" (Jn 8:12). He was speaking to the crowds gathered in the Temple. Nearby stood four seventy-five foot tall menorahs lit for the feast. Their brilliant light bathed the whole city of Jerusalem. Their light reminded the people of the pillar of fire which guided Israel through the journey to the Promised Land. In saying that He is the Light of the world, Jesus is claiming that He is the true light that guides all people along the path to salvation.

On another occasion, during the Feast of Dedication, known today as Hanukkah, Jesus proclaimed, "I am the door (θύρα). Anyone who enters through me will be saved. He will go in and out and will find pasture" (Jn 10:9). Just as sheep enter into the sheepfold through its door and find safe shelter, all who enter the kingdom through Christ the Good Shepherd are not only safe but are saved.

No matter how hemmed in we may be, Jesus is the way to peace, even amid the trials of this life. No matter how harried we are from our work, Jesus is the way to rest, even in the midst of our labors. No matter how sorely beset we are by temptations, He is the way to victory. Entering through the door who is Christ means entering into union with Him who is our peace and reconciliation. Jesus Himself is the narrow door through which we enter the kingdom of God. Through Him passes no self-righteous individual, no one filled with self-glory, no pompous or proud person. Only those who make themselves little in their own eyes can squeeze through the narrow entrance. Like the Holy Roman Emperor Henry IV at Canossa, we are kept outside the kingdom of God until we lay down our tinsel crowns and take off our royal robes and stand clothed only in the hair shirt of penitence.

In saying that He is the door, Jesus vividly expresses a central truth of the Christian faith. He alone is "the way, the truth and the life" (Jn 14:6). Only through Him is salvation possible. Jesus' claim is exclusive. Today it is rejected by those who hold that Buddha, Confucius, Moses, Jesus, and Muhammad mapped out different roads to God and it does not matter what road someone takes. But it does matter!

The Buddha, Siddhartha Gautama, taught that salvation was nirvana. Being saved meant achieving the ultimate state of release from continual reincarnations and the extinction of individual consciousness. At the age of 80, the Buddha died of food poisoning and was buried.

Confucius was a philosopher interested in changing society for the better. He never measured up to his own standards. He died at the age of 73 and was buried. He left behind to his followers no set beliefs about the afterlife.

Moses was God's chosen instrument. He planted monotheism in the soul of the Chosen People. He led

The Parable of the Narrow Door 123

them from slavery in Egypt to freedom in their own land. He died and was buried on Mt. Nebo.

Muhammad founded Islam and promoted belief in one God. He had eleven wives at one time, along with a number of concubines. He waged many a military campaign to spread his teachings. At 62, he died in the arms of Aisha, his favorite wife, and was buried.

Jesus preached His gospel of love and forgiveness. He healed the sick and cast out demons. He raised from the dead the daughter of Jairus, the son of the widow of Nain, and his friend Lazarus. He claimed to be God. At the age of 33, abandoned by His followers, He died on a cross and was buried in a borrowed tomb. Three days later, Jesus rose from the dead. His followers worship Him as God.

Just as the lives and deaths of the founders of the major religions differ, so do the religions they started. People who say that all religions lead to the one God also claim that it does not matter what road you take. But Jesus says otherwise. "No one comes to the Father except through me" (Jn 14:6).

"God wills everyone to be saved and to come to knowledge of the truth" (1 Tim 2:4). He has given us the way to be saved in Christ Jesus, "the one mediator between God and the human race" (1 Tim 2:5). We do not create our own way to God. Christ is the way. He is the one Mediator between God and us. Christ is the one Redeemer. By His Death and Resurrection, He redeems all people of every time and place. All who are saved are saved because Jesus gave Himself as a "ransom for all" (1 Tim 2:6).

There is an essential relationship between Christ as Savior and the Church as the instrument of salvation for all. "The Lord Jesus, the only Savior, did not only establish a simple community of disciples, but constituted the

Church as a salvific mystery: he himself is in the Church and the Church is in him (Jn 15:1ff; Gal 3:28; Eph 4:15-16; Acts 9:5). Therefore, the fullness of Christ's salvific mystery belongs also to the Church, inseparably united to her Lord" (*Dominus Jesus*, 16).

Christ is now present to us in His Body, which is the Church, as the one Mediator and the unique way of salvation. Thus, the Church, which Christ Himself founded, is necessary for salvation (*Lumen Gentium*, 14). "All grace comes from Christ the Head through the Church which is his Body" (*Catechism of the Catholic Church*, 846). This is a truth that many simply do not accept. They fear that accepting this truth excludes non-Catholics from the possibility of salvation.

The truth that all grace, all salvation, comes from Christ, whose Body is the Church, needs to be seen together with another truth of the faith. Yes, God has made the Church the very instrument to bring all people into relationship with the Paschal Mystery. However, God accomplishes this in mysterious ways. As the Second Vatican Council taught,

> All this holds true not only for Christians, but for all men of good will in whose hearts grace works in an unseen way. For, since Christ died for all men, and since the ultimate vocation of man is in fact one, and divine, we ought to believe that the Holy Spirit in a manner known only to God offers to every man the possibility of being associated with this Paschal Mystery. *Gaudium et Spes*, 22

Once Peter Seewald, a German journalist and avowed atheist, interviewed Cardinal Ratzinger (the future Pope Benedict XVI). He sought his views on a variety of thorny and controversial theological issues. When he asked him

The Parable of the Narrow Door

how many ways were there to God, Cardinal Ratzinger spoke with candor and profound insight.

> As many as there are people. For, even within the same faith, each man's way is an entirely personal one. We have Christ's word: I am the way. In that respect, there is ultimately one way, and, everyone who is on the way to God is therefore in some sense also on the way of Jesus Christ. But this does not mean that all ways are identical in terms of consciousness and will, but, on the contrary, the one way is so big that it becomes a personal way for each man. *Salt of the Earth*, p. 32

God works in His own mysterious way to offer His grace to all. "Oh, the depth of the riches and wisdom and knowledge of God! How inscrutable are his judgments and how unsearchable his ways!" (Rom 11:33)

In Luke's gospel, after teaching the very brief parable of the Narrow Door, Jesus goes on to give another parable.

> When once the master of the house has gotten up and shut the door, you may find yourself standing outside knocking on the door and begging, "Lord, open the door for us." He will say in reply, "I do not know where you come from." Then you will protest, "We ate and drank with you, and you taught in our streets." But he will say, "I do not know where you come from. Depart from me, all you evildoers!"
>
> There will be weeping and gnashing of teeth when you see Abraham and Isaac and Jacob and all the Prophets in the kingdom of God as you yourselves are being thrown out. Then from the east and the west, and from the north and the south, people will come and take their places at the banquet in the

kingdom of God. Indeed some are last who will be first, and some are first who will be last.

Lk 13:25-30

This passage sounds very much like a composite of material taken from the Sermon on the Mount in Matthew 7:22, from the parable of the Ten Virgins in Matthew 25:10-12, and from the healing of the centurion's servant in Matthew 8:11-14. Luke had access to this material as did Matthew. However, he brought it all together and appended it to the parable of the Narrow Door, even though this material originally circulated independently. He did this for two reasons.

First, Luke wishes to re-echo the teaching of Jesus in the parable of the Ten Virgins. In that parable, the bridegroom arrives unexpectedly when the lamps of five foolish virgins have gone out. The oil of the other five cannot be given to them, because the oil symbolizes good works done in love and these cannot be credited to another. In the parable, the bridegroom's arrival symbolizes the moment of death when, with hearts full of love shared in good deeds, we either join the Lord for the nuptials of heaven and earth or we are excluded.

At that moment, "at the evening of life, we shall be judged on our love" (St. John of the Cross, *Dichos* 64). If we do not love others as Christ loves us, then the door to the kingdom of heaven will be shut and entrance barred. It is then that our eternal destiny is sealed. But, until then, God keeps the door open, beckoning us to enter.

Second, Luke wishes us not to limit the number of those who will be saved. In the appended material, Jesus uses the very popular image of heaven as a banquet with Abraham, Isaac, and Jacob. He alludes to both Isaiah 45:6 and Isaiah 49:12. These two passages speak of people coming to salvation from all four corners of the world to the feast of heaven.

In this added material, Jesus also makes an unmistakable reference to Isaiah's vision of the banquet prepared by God for all people.

> On this mountain the Lord of hosts
> will prepare for all peoples
> a feast of rich food and choice wines,
> of succulent foods and well-aged wines.
> On this mountain the Lord will destroy
> the veil that shrouds all the peoples,
> the path spread over all the nations.   *Isa 25:6-7*

Isaiah looks forward to a time when Israel and the Gentiles will feast together. No race or nation is excluded. All are called to salvation. "Greek and Jew, circumcision and uncircumcision, barbarian, Scythian, slave, free" are equally invited (Col 3:11). Isaiah's vision points to the marriage feast of the Lamb with "a great multitude, which no one could count, from every nation, race, people, and language" (Rev 7:9).

The narrow door parable and the appended parable of the householder closing the door taken together are Jesus' complete response to those curious about the number of the saved. How many will they be? Too numerous to count! Jesus does not want us to waste our energy putting limits on God's mercy. Rather, He desires us to open our lives here and now to God's offer of salvation.

Martin Luther, the father of Protestantism, is often quoted as saying that there will be three surprises for all who get to heaven. First, there will be people in heaven we did not expect to be there. Second, there will be people not present in heaven we thought for sure would be there. And, the third and greatest surprise of all: we ourselves are there!

CHAPTER 10

The Parable of the Prodigal Son

Between the Temple Mount and the Mount of Olives in Jerusalem lies the Valley of Jehoshaphat. Here, according to the prophet Joel, God will judge the entire world (Joel 4:1-2). From ancient times, many pious families have buried their dead in this valley waiting for the resurrection from the dead on the Day of Judgment. Among the many tombs crowding this cemetery is the Tomb of Absalom. It is a Hellenistic burial monument, rising 47 feet and clearly visible above the valley floor. History, legend, and custom make this tomb stand out from all the others.

Absalom, the third son of King David, was his only son with royal blood from both his father and his mother. His good looks and charm won him the favor of his father and the admiration of the young aristocrats of the royal city. But his life was anything but favored.

Absalom's story reads like a sordid tragedy of human weakness: lust, incest, deceit, grief, rage, revenge, rebellion, and betrayal. When David failed to take revenge for the rape of Absalom's sister Tamar, Absalom took matters into his own hands. A leader with great charisma, he led a revolt against his father, but failed. David's general, Joab, killed him in battle. His death caused David profound grief. With loud sobs and laments, David cried aloud, "Would that I had died in place of you. O, Absalom, my son, my son" (2 Sam 18:33).

The broken heart of King David faintly mirrors the wounded heart of the Father who never ceases to love us when we rebel against Him by our sins. That which

The Parable of the Prodigal Son

David could not do, God did. On the Cross, Jesus, who is truly God, took our place and died for our sins so that we might live.

Over the centuries, there developed a curious custom around the Tomb of Absalom. Jews, Christians, and Muslims began to bring their unruly children there. They would make them throw stones at the monument of the son who had raised his hand against his father. Thus, parents gave their children an unforgettable lesson of the fate of children who rebel against their parents.

From the writings of the Jewish historian Josephus, we know that the Tomb of Absalom was well known in the first century. On his visits to Jerusalem, Jesus passed by it many times. No doubt, He saw it with His eyes and remembered in His heart the famous passage in Deuteronomy that speaks about the fate of a rebellious son.

> If someone has a stubborn and rebellious son who will not listen to his father or his mother, and will not heed them even when he is disciplined, then his father and mother are to take hold of him and bring him out to the elders at the town gate. They are to say to the town elders, "This son of ours is stubborn and rebellious. He will not listen to us. He is a glutton and a drunkard." Then all the men of that town will stone him to death. You must purge the evil from your midst. All of Israel will hear of it and be filled with fear. *Deut 21:18-21*

This law is harsh. But, in the context of the times, it was seen as an expression of justice. In ancient societies, the father was the law. In fact, in the *Code of Hammurabi* (n. 168, 169), the father had absolute power over his son's life. Not so in biblical law. The father could not be judge, jury, and executioner.

A father whose relationship with his son had gone bad could not simply do away with him. Along with his wife, he had to bring the case before the elders of the city. Since the elders certainly would have been familiar with both the parents and the son, they were in a position to limit any harm that an angry father would be tempted to inflict on his son. Thus, the law actually was a protection of the rights of a son accused of rebellion.

Jesus knew Deuteronomy. He quotes it in His teachings more than any other book in the Pentateuch. He certainly knew this passage very well, for He uses it as the raw material for His poignant parable of the Prodigal Son.

Whereas Deuteronomy had moved parents away from anger and revenge to justice, Jesus goes beyond justice to mercy. In Jesus' parable of the Prodigal Son (Lk 15), the younger son squanders "his inheritance on a life of disolute living" (Lk 15:13). He swallows up "the father's money with loose women" (Lk 15:30). He is "a glutton and a drunkard," just as Deuteronomy describes (Deut 21:20).

Of all the parables that Jesus ever told, the parable of the Prodigal Son stands out as the most memorable. It is sometimes called the parable of the Loving Father. For both the rebellion of the younger son and the reluctance of the elder brother to forgive his brother do not diminish the father's love for both. This image of the father in the parable emphasizes Jesus' teaching of an all-loving God who "makes his sun rise on the bad and the good, and causes rain to fall on the just and the unjust" (Mt 5:45). This parable is one of the greatest love stories ever told.

> Then he said: "There was a man who had two sons. The younger of them said to his father, 'Father, give me the share of your estate that I will inherit.' And so the father divided the property between them.

The Parable of the Prodigal Son

A few days later the younger son gathered together everything he had and traveled to a distant country, where he squandered his inheritance on a life of dissolute living. When he had spent it all, a severe famine afflicted that country, and he began to be in need. So he went and hired himself out to one of the local inhabitants who sent him to his farm to feed the pigs. He would have willingly filled his stomach with the pods that the pigs were eating, but no one gave him anything.

Then he came to his senses and said, 'How many of my father's hired workers have more food than they can consume, while here I am, dying of hunger. I will depart from this place and go to my father, and I will say to him, "Father, I have sinned against heaven and against you. I am no longer worthy to be called your son. Treat me like one of your hired workers."'

So he set out for his father's house. But while he was still a long way off, his father saw him and was filled with compassion. He ran to him, threw his arms around him, and kissed him. Then the son said to him, 'Father, I have sinned against heaven and against you. I am no longer worthy to be called your son.'

But the father said to his servants, 'Quickly bring out the finest robe we have and put it on him. Place a ring on his finger and sandals on his feet. Then bring the fatted calf and kill it, and let us celebrate with a feast. For this son of mine was dead and has come back to life. He was lost, and now he has been found.' And they began to celebrate.

Now the elder son had been out in the fields, and as he returned and drew near the house, he could hear the sounds of music and dancing. He summoned one of the servants and inquired what all this meant. The servant replied, 'Your brother has come home, and your father has killed the fatted calf because he has him back safe and sound.' The elder son then became angry and refused to go in. His father came out and began to plead with him, but he said to his father in reply, 'All these years I have worked like a slave for you, and I never once disobeyed your orders. Even so, you have never even given me a young goat so that I might celebrate with my friends. But when this son of yours returns after wasting his inheritance from you on prostitutes, you kill the fatted calf for him.'

Then the father said to him, 'Son, you are with me always, and everything I have is yours. But it was only right that we should celebrate and rejoice, because this brother of yours was dead and has come to life; he was lost and now he has been found.' " *Lk 15:11-32*

Jesus tells this parable on an occasion when the Pharisees and scribes are distressed by His outreach to sinners. "The tax collectors and sinners were all drawing near to listen to him, but the Pharisees and scribes began to complain, saying, 'This man welcomes sinners and eats with them'" (Lk 15:2). Rabbis of the first century kept a distance from sinners. These religious leaders looked upon sinners as hopelessly lost. But not Jesus. He welcomes them. When others turn their face away from us because of our sins, Jesus opens His arms and beckons us to come to Him.

In the parable, when the younger son demands his share of the inheritance, he is not merely asserting his youthful independence. To desire independence is good.

The Parable of the Prodigal Son

But, when our independence severs the bonds of love and rightful authority, disaster ensues.

In the culture of the time, the inheritance was passed on to the sons at the time of the father's death. A son demanding his share *before* his father's death was publicly declaring the father as good as dead. As St. Peter Chrysologus says, "The son is weary of his father's own life. Since he cannot shorten his father's life, he works to get possession of his property."

Selfishly taking his share of the inheritance, he leaves home. He is thinking only of himself. He rejects the communion of life and love that should exist between himself and his father. In the words of Deuteronomy, he is truly "stubborn and rebellious."

In the prophet Hosea, God says of His rebellious child Israel, "How could I give you up...or deliver you up? My heart is overwhelmed...My pity is stirred. I will not give vent to my fierce anger. For I am God and not a mortal" (Hos 11:8-9). In the father of the Prodigal Son, word becomes deed.

Eventually need drives the prodigal home. When the younger son returns home, his father sees him coming from far off. The father has been anxiously hoping for this moment. His eyes have grown weary searching the horizon for his son. The father is the first to see him and he runs to him, overjoyed.

In the culture of Jesus' day, no man of standing would be seen running. Pulling up his robe and running in view of others would bring shame and dishonor. In the parable, there is a reason why the father casts off his dignity to run and meet his son.

When a Jewish man who had lived among Gentiles and had lost his wealth, returned to his village, the moment he arrived at the city gates, the elders of the community would go to meet him in order to perform the *kezazah* ceremony. They would break a large clay pot in front of him, symbolizing the broken relationship between the sinner and the community. In an act of total rejection, they would shout, "You are now cut off from your people!"

In the parable of the Prodigal Son, the father wants to get to his son before the elders. He does not want his returning son to be cut off from him. He runs to embrace him in full view of all.

The law of Deuteronomy required that the rebellious son be stoned to death at the city gates. The father reaches his son while he is still away from home. He holds on to him in love so that the others are not able to carry out what the law demanded in justice. God's mercy always goes beyond what justice requires and grants forgiveness to the repentant. Our contrition may not always be perfect, but God's love is!

In Jesus' parable, the son does not need to grovel before his father and plead for forgiveness, as would have been expected. No! The father runs to meet his son before the elders. He does not reject his son and he would have no one else reject him. Hastening, breathless, with tunic tucked up and bare legs exposed, he shames himself so that his son does not experience the shame of the community. What a moving image of God!

In Christ Crucified, God the Son runs to us. His arms are outstretched even to welcome the nails that pierce His hands. In the ignominy of the Cross, God has taken our shame to Himself. Jesus is stripped of His clothes and all dignity so that we might be clothed in grace and receive the dignity of being the sons and daughters of God.

The Parable of the Prodigal Son

Driven by an emptiness in his heart more painful than the gnawing hunger in his stomach, the prodigal returns home. He rehearses again and again his painful confession: "Father, I have sinned against heaven and against you. I am no longer worthy to be called your son. Treat me as you would treat one of your hired workers" (Lk 15:18-19). His father's joyful embrace cuts short his well-prepared speech. He is not to be treated like a hired servant. In God's eyes, we are more than servants (Jn 15:15). In baptism, we put on Christ and truly become His children.

The father embraces his son, holding him close to his heart, kissing him again and again as would a mother showering affection on her child. What a great image of God that Jesus gives us! God transcends our categories. He who is Father has within His bosom a mother's heart.

Jesus knew well the words of the prophet Isaiah, "As a mother comforts her child, so will I comfort you." (Isa 66:13). Lamenting over Jerusalem and our sinful hearts, Jesus said, "How often have I longed to gather [you] together as a hen gathers her chicks under her wings, but you were unwilling!" (Lk 13:34). God yearns for our repentance. "Repentance raises again the fallen soul, lifts up the destitute, heals the broken" (St. John Chrysostom).

God reckons the forgiveness of our sins as His honor. When God forgives, it is not for anything in us. Rather, as He says through the prophet Isaiah, "It is I, who blot out your transgressions for my own sake, and I will remember your sins no more" (Isa 43:25). For the glory of His name, he forgives our sins (Isa 48:9). Like the mist dissipated by the rising sun, God's mercy dispels our sins and makes us wholly alive to His love. For, as St. Irenaeus said, "the glory of God is man fully alive."

With a heavy dose of self-pity, the elder brother in Jesus' parable becomes angry when he is told that the father has welcomed back his brother. Reminding his father of the enormity of his brother's rebellion, he complains, "Look, all these years I served you and not once did I disobey your orders; yet you never gave me even a young goat to feast on with my friends. But when your son returns who swallowed up your property with prostitutes, for him you slaughter the fattened calf."

The elder brother disowns his younger brother before the father. With the phrase "this son of yours," he echoes the words of the parents in Deuteronomy disowning their rebellious son before the elders with the words "This son of ours." Every sin we commit, even our most secret sin, diminishes our relationship with others. Every member of our family suffers when we turn away from God. The rebellious heart directed away from God is never simply a personal matter with individual consequences alone.

The same love that the father shows the younger son, he extends to the elder brother. Both sons are sinners. The younger by rebellion. The elder by jealousy. When he refuses to join in celebrating his younger brother's return, the father comes to him, pleading for him to put aside his animosity and to welcome his brother. To his selfish insistence on his own rights, the father tenderly gives a gentle reprimand, "My son, you are here with me always; everything I have is yours."

The elder brother in the parable is the Pharisees and scribes to whom Jesus addresses this parable. Like the elder brother, they gloried in their scrupulous observance of the law. Each of them could say with the elder brother, "All these years I served you and not once did I disobey your orders."

The Parable of the Prodigal Son

The Pharisees and scribes saw their relationship to God as that of servant to king. They were self-righteous. They were proud of their obedient service. But Jesus came to change our understanding of God and our relationship with Him. We are not God's servants. We are God's children. He is the Father who longs for us to love Him.

Unlike the younger brother who represents the sinners Jesus welcomes, the Pharisees and scribes acknowledged no sin. As the Venerable Archbishop Sheen once said, "The worst thing in the world is not sin, it is denying that we are sinners. Sinners who deny that there is sin, deny thereby the remedy of sin, and thus cut themselves off forever from him who came to redeem."

The parable concludes without an ending. The father is standing on the doorstep, inviting the elder son to enter and to celebrate the joy of being one family. His heart is aching for the elder son to complete his joy. He is waiting for this son's response.

Jesus deliberately does not tell us what the elder son chooses to do. He is speaking to His critics, inviting them to be seated at table with Him and sinners, celebrating the joy of being one family. The door is open. He waits for their response. He waits for ours.

The story Jesus masterfully tells in the parable of the Prodigal Son also reveals something of the mystery of Jesus Himself. As Jesus enters His passion, He leaves the Last Supper. He walks across the Kidron Valley with the disciples to the Garden of Gethsemane. In the full light of the Passover moon, His eyes come to rest upon the Tomb of Absalom. He remembers the law of Deuteronomy. According to this law, the elders of the city are to carry out a death sentence for the rebellious son who was "a glutton and a drunkard" (Deut 21:20).

"A glutton and a drunkard:" this is how Jesus' enemies have labeled Him. His ministry has been so different from that of the Baptist. No fire. No brimstone. But mercy and forgiveness. He ate and drank with sinners.

To those meticulously keeping the law, he has said, "The tax collectors and the prostitutes are entering the kingdom of God ahead of you" (Mt 21:31). And so they complained, "Look, he is a glutton and a drunkard, a friend of tax collectors and sinners" (Mt 11:19). They judged Him the rebellious son of Israel. For, in their eyes, He was squandering the rich inheritance of the law on sinners.

Jesus knows that His life on earth is about to end on the Cross. Three times during His public ministry, He had predicted it (Mk 9:31; 10:32-34). At the Last Supper, He interprets the meaning of His impending death. He is the Suffering Servant of Isaiah, who takes on Himself the sins of others (Isa 53:8). As St. Paul says, "For our sake he made him who did not know sin to be sin, so that through him we might become the righteousness of God" (2 Cor 5:21). Jesus is all of us, the prodigal, empty, beaten, and stripped of dignity, because of our sins.

Recognizing what was ahead, Jesus enters the Garden of Gethsemane. He prays beneath its gnarled olive trees, even as the elders, with a twisted sense of justice, plot to put Him to death. The weight of our sins crushes Him to the ground. But He rises with purpose and courage.

Jesus goes to the Cross, taking upon Himself our sins. He is the Son who knows the infinite mercy of the Father who says, "This son of mine was dead and has come to life. He was lost, and now he has been found" (Lk 15:24). The road to Golgotha is the way to glory. Jesus "humbled himself, becoming obedient to death, even death on a cross. Because of this, God greatly exalted him and bestowed on him the name that is above all other names" (Phil 2:8-9).

The Cross of Jesus is the return of the Prodigal Son, that is, all of us, into the home of our Father. In the Crucified Christ, we encounter the Father who runs to meet us. In Christ's arms stretched out on the Cross, the Father embraces us with His love.

Even as we try to utter our words of repentance, His love overwhelms us. He invites us to enter His house and to take our place at the table. At every Eucharist, we already share in the eternal banquet of the Lamb where one day we will know a joy that never ends.

The parable of the Prodigal Son gives us insight into God's merciful will to save. It perfectly expresses in a narrative what Jesus did for us in deed. He blotted out our sins through His Passion, Death, and Resurrection and restored us to our rightful place in the Father's house. May our reflection on this parable lead us to lift our hearts in prayer with the words of Sacred Scripture: "Blessed be the God and Father of our Lord Jesus Christ. In his great mercy he has given us a new birth to a living hope through the resurrection of Jesus Christ from the dead" (1 Pet 1:3).

CHAPTER 11

The Parable of the Pharisee and the Publican

Perched on Mount Moriah where God commanded Abraham to sacrifice his beloved son Isaac, Solomon built the Temple in Jerusalem. Centuries later, Herod rebuilt and expanded it. The Jewish historian Flavius Josephus lavishes unrestrained praises on its beauty. "... The building wanted nothing that could astound either mind or eye. For, being covered on all sides with massive plates of gold, the sun was no sooner up than it radiated so fiery a flash that persons straining to look at it were compelled to avert their eyes, as from the solar rays. ...All that was not overlaid with gold was of the purest white" (Ant. 15.391-395).

In this magnificent Temple, every day at 9 a.m., the priest would place a sacrificed lamb on the fires of the altar. Again in the evening at 3 p.m., the priest would sacrifice another male lamb on top of all the offerings made during the day on that same altar. This second lamb stayed smoldering on the altar for the entire night. The next morning the priest would remove the ashes and repeat the same ceremonies. In this way, there was *olah tamid*, a continuous burnt offering, a perpetual sacrifice, to the Lord (Ex 29:38-46).

In Jesus' day, pious Jews would go to pray during the morning and evening sacrifice offered in the Temple. Like other faithful Jews, Jesus and His own disciples followed this custom (Acts 2:15; 3:1). On many occasions, Jesus not only took in the sight of the many gathered for prayer, but He also noticed the individuals among them. From His astute observation of human nature, He told the short, but poignant parable of the Pharisee and Publican.

The Parable of the Pharisee and the Publican

He also told the following parable to some people who prided themselves about their own righteousness and regarded others with contempt: "Two men went up to the temple to pray. One was a Pharisee and the other was a tax collector. The Pharisee stood up and said this prayer to himself: 'I thank you, God, that I am not like other people—greedy, dishonest, adulterous—or even like this tax collector. I fast twice a week and pay tithes on all my income.'

The tax collector, however, stood some distance away and would not even raise his eyes to heaven. Rather, he kept beating his breast as he said, 'God, be merciful to me, a sinner.' This man, I tell you, returned to his home justified, whereas the other did not. For everyone who exalts himself will be humbled, but the one who humbles himself will be exalted."
Lk 18:9-14

In his gospel, St. Luke places this parable immediately after the parable of the Persistent Widow (Lk 18:1-8). The evangelist offers that parable as an example of "the necessity...to pray always and never to lose heart" (Lk 18:1). As a result, many understand the parable of the Pharisee and the Publican as a further instruction on prayer.

Thus, Jesus would be teaching that those who truly know the infinite greatness of God are always humble. When they come before God in prayer, their humility opens the path to the throne of grace. Certainly, the very last line of the parable would favor this interpretation. Jesus truly valued humility in the way He lived. For, in every circumstance of life, "humility and knowledge in poor clothes excel pride and ignorance in costly attire" (William Penn). But the parable is not just about humility.

In His ongoing dialogue with the Pharisees who did not understand Jesus' constant outreach to sinners, Jesus tells the parable of the Pharisee and the Publican who go up to the Temple to pray. While speaking of the way both individuals pray, Jesus is addressing an even deeper issue. He begins the parable by speaking of prayer. He ends the parable by teaching the very nature of redemption.

Luke's label on this parable tells us that it was spoken to the very people who were represented in it by the Pharisee. One can fancy their faces as they listened to Jesus. Their self-righteousness made them more hostile to Him.

In the parable, Jesus captures the antagonism between the Pharisees and the tax collectors. The Pharisees formed a religious-political group with great moral influence. The Pharisees devoted themselves to studying the Torah and to keeping its many commandments.

The Pharisees were so fearful of transgressing the Law that they put a hedge around it, i.e., other observances that would distance them from even the possibility of breaking a commandment (Mk 7:1-16). Jesus often engaged in heated debate with them on such issues as fasting, divorce, and Sabbath observance. Nonetheless, He was friendly enough with them to be invited to their homes for dinner (Lk 7:36; 11:37; 14:1).

The tax collectors paid greater allegiance to Caesar than to Moses. Not so observant of the Torah, they obeyed for their own profit the law of Rome. They exacted taxes and tolls for their Roman oppressors. Since they paid a certain sum of the money from what they collected into the Roman treasury (*publicum*), they were called "publicans."

It was not uncommon for them to cheat their fellow Jews. They would extort more than was due Rome, keep-

The Parable of the Pharisee and the Publican

ing the extra for themselves. They would also threaten imprisonment for those who did not cooperate. No wonder they were so universally despised.

In the parable, the Pharisee prides himself on keeping the law. He trusted in his own goodness as the source of his righteousness. He represents the many other Pharisees who sincerely believed that their obedience to even the smallest details of the law earned them the right to be justified in God's eyes. The tax-collector stands for all those whom the Pharisees judged sinners, because they did not or could not keep the many laws that the Pharisees did.

Many who gathered around Jesus were Pharisees. They were good men, eager to hear Jesus speak. His fresh approach and His deep insights at first intrigued them. Eventually, many of them turned against Him, because He so freely welcomed sinners and tax collectors (Mt 9:11).

In the parable, both the Pharisee and the tax collector go up to the Temple to pray. All are welcome in God's house. Many people come to church, because they can hear a good homily, listen to uplifting music, or experience community. All these reasons are good in themselves. Sadly, however, when some people are not satisfied with the homily or the music or the sense of community, they leave disappointed, sometimes not returning.

We should never forget the principal reason for going to church. We go to offer our prayers of praise and thanksgiving. As we pray in the words of the preface to the Eucharist Prayer, "It is truly right and just, our duty and our salvation, always and everywhere to give thanks..." We go primarily to give worship to God, not to get something for ourselves.

The Pharisee and tax collector go to pray at the moment of public worship. The Pharisee distances himself from the crowd in the Temple court. According to the Mishnah, if a righteous person even brushed against the clothes of those who did not keep the law, he became unclean. And so the Pharisee deliberately stands alone.

In his mind, there are only two kinds of people in the world: the righteous and the unrighteous. He belongs to the former. He is better than everyone else. His pride in his own accomplishments separates him from all others and causes his spiritual downfall. As St. Augustine once taught, "it was pride that turned angels into devils: it is humility that makes men angels."

The tax collector also stands apart from the crowd. He judges himself as unrighteous. His humility makes him avoid being near the other worshipers. He sees himself as unworthy to join them. He is content just to be in the presence of God, even at a distance. His very position is a prayer itself exclaiming, "Better to spend one day in your courts than a thousand elsewhere. I would rather be a doorkeeper in God's house than dwell inside the tents of the wicked" (Ps 84:11).

How important is the House of God, the place where God chooses to dwell! Before all His works of creation, we stand in awe at the power and beauty, the grandeur and goodness of God. But, in church, we are in the very presence of God. The church is the "temple sacred in the Lord...[it is all of us] being built together into a dwelling place of God in the Spirit" (Eph 2:22). In that sacred place, through the preaching of the Word and the sacraments, God enriches us with His blessings, strengthens us with His grace and crowns our lives with His mercy.

Even as pious Jews do today at the Western Wall in Jerusalem, the Pharisee in the parable utters his prayer out

The Parable of the Pharisee and the Publican

loud. His words reek of the stench of self-praise and pride. He says, "O God, I thank you that I am not like the rest of humanity—greedy, dishonest, adulterous—or even like this tax collector." Far from being a prayer to God, his words are a ruthless attack on the tax collector. Instead of praising and thanking God, he is accusing and judging another of sin. In fact, only his first word even mentions God.

Nothing is more abhorrent to God than the person who glibly condemns another person of sin. Worse still the person who destroys the name of a good person. In the end, the one "who does not believe others virtuous, would be found, were the secrets of his heart and life known, to be himself vicious" (T. Guthrie). In the words of the good thief crucified with Jesus, such a person has no fear of God. He does not recognize that all of us are under the same condemnation (Lk 23:40). "All have sinned and are deprived of the glory of God" (Rom 3:23).

Those who make it their business to publicize the sins of others close themselves off from God's grace. Recognizing one's own sins and not those of others is the prerequisite to forgiveness. "Do not judge and you will not be judged. Do not condemn, and you will not be condemned. Forgive, and you will be forgiven" (Lk 6:37).

We use our conscience well when we examine our own soul, not focusing on the splinter in another's eye while ignoring the wooden beam in our own (Lk 6:41). Pride makes culprits of those who lash out at others in their personal crusade for justice and yet are woefully negligent of honesty about themselves. Their rebuke of others is ludicrous.

After attacking his fellow worshiper, the Pharisee lists his own acts of righteousness. Moses mandated a fast for the Day of Atonement. But this Pharisee fasts twice a week. He tithes not just the produce of his land as required but his whole income. He goes beyond the law and boasts for all to hear of his good deeds. The Pharisee is not a humble man bowing before God. In the twenty-nine words on his lips in the Greek text, five times he says *I*; only once does he say *God*. As St. Bernard notes, he is not so much thankful for being righteous as for being alone in his goodness. There is not a hint of true devotion in his soliloquy.

Jesus needs only a few words to paint for us His portrait of the tax collector. Only one verse. His body language speaks volumes. He does not even raise his eyes to heaven, as was the custom when praying. Nor does he raise his hands. Instead, he keeps beating his breast with his fists. This is a very unusual gesture for a man in Jesus' day. It is an expression of deep sorrow usually done by women. The tax collector is truly repentant.

His *mea culpa* goes straight to the heart, the source of all evil. "For from the heart come evil thoughts, murder, adultery, fornication, theft, perjury, blasphemy. These are the things that defile a person..." (Mt 15:19-20). His dramatic gesture of beating his breast expresses in deed the prayer of David "Create in me a clean heart, O God" (Ps 51:12).

Keenly aware of his own sins, he prays with utter earnestness. The only thing he says about himself is that he is a sinner. No need to argue his case before the divine Judge who knows the secrets of our hearts. "God does not see the way that men see, for men look on the outward appearance, but the Lord looks at the heart" (1 Sam 16:7). No need for long prayers. He simply says, "O God, be merciful to me a sinner."

Bartimaeus, the blind beggar who encounters Jesus on His last journey to Jerusalem, cries out, "Have mercy on me." The tax-collector also begs for mercy. But, in speak-

The Parable of the Pharisee and the Publican

ing to Jesus, he uses a different expression. He literally says, "make atonement for me" (ἱλάσθητί μοι: hilasthēti). This word "to make atonement" (ἱλάσκομαι: hilaskomai) is found nowhere else in the gospels. It is found, however, in Hebrews 2:17 where Jesus, our merciful High Priest, is said to make atonement (hilaskomai) for the sins of the people. Paul even calls Jesus our atonement (ἱλαστήριον: hilastērion; Rom 3:25).

The very same word ἱλαστήριον (hilastērion) is used in the Greek Old Testament for the mercy seat, i.e., the lid or covering of the ark which the high priest sprinkled with the blood of the sacrificial victim on the Day of Atonement. Since Luke was a close companion of Paul, he may have heard Paul, so well-versed in the Old Testament, speak of Jesus as our atonement. And so, when it comes to recording the tax-collector's prayer, Luke frames his plea for mercy in a way to remind us that Christ is the mercy seat of the New Covenant.

In his brief petition for mercy, the tax collector recognizes that he himself can do nothing to repair his broken relationship with God. Only God can. And God does.

In Christ Crucified, God heals our broken relationship with Him. On the Cross, Jesus makes the perfect atonement for our sins, restoring us to grace. Thus, we poor sinners can have confidence even in our weakness. For, "if anyone does sin, we have an Advocate with the Father, Jesus Christ the righteous one. He is atonement (ἱλασμός: hilasmos) for our sins, and not for our sins only but for those of the whole world" (1 Jn 2:1-2).

The tax collector, burdened with the weight of his own sins, offers his brief prayer for mercy in humility and trust. God immediately responds. He forgives him. At this point, Jesus abruptly ends the parable.

The two men went up to the Temple together, first the Pharisee, then the publican. Now they leave the Temple in reverse order. The tax collector goes first, because God has heard his prayer and has justified him. The Pharisee lags behind. Not only has God not justified him, but his prayer has placed him in a worse spiritual state than he was in before. He could not be forgiven, because he did not admit his sin.

Our modern society no longer believes in sin. It jettisons the moral law. It refuses to accept it as a standard for good and evil. As a result, it is sinning more and more and admitting it less and less. How often people simply say that everyone goes to heaven. Why? Because there is no sin to keep them out. When God is banished from a secularistic society, how can anything ever be an offense against Him? No God. No moral law. No sin. Only a society left to its own depravity.

We who believe in Jesus are not left alone in our sins. His gospel is glad tidings of great joy for *sinners*. His very name "Jesus" means "God saves." "Once united with the Crucified..., we begin to understand that everywhere else others promise us sin excused, sin discounted, sin denied, sin explained away, but only at the foot of the Cross do we ever experience the beautiful divine contradiction of sin forgiven" (Archbishop Fulton Sheen).

For many in today's world, it may take some time before they can cry out with the tax collector, "O God, make atonement for me, a sinner." But when we do, there is forgiveness of our sins, healing for our broken spirit and ointment for our wounds. A better future always begins with the tears of repentance.

CHAPTER 12

The Parable of the Great Banquet

On July 6, 1483, some three thousand people gathered in Westminster Hall, London to celebrate the coronation of Richard III as King of England. The most important royal dignitaries sat down to a lavish banquet of multiple courses. Others packed galleries just to watch the festivities. Sharing a meal has always symbolized sharing life; and, being invited to the royal table, a recognition of fidelity and a reward for service. A banquet given by a king is not just a meal and a meal provided by God is always a royal feast.

From the very first pages of Sacred Scripture to the last, God shows His love and compassion by providing food for humankind. In the biblical account of creation, God does not simply create Adam and Eve. He cares for them and provides the very food they are to eat. To our first parents, God says, "Behold, I give you every plant that produces seeds upon the earth and every tree that has fruit with its seed inside of it; these shall be your food…" (Gen 1:29). And, on the final pages of Scripture, God calls His people to the fullness of joy in the wedding feast of the Lamb (Rev 19:7-10).

In the Old Testament, the prophet Isaiah looked forward to the day when God would bring to completion His plan for salvation. Then He will offer the messianic banquet. Isaiah predicted that, at the end of time, when God's enemies and death itself are destroyed, "the Lord of hosts will provide for all peoples a feast of rich food and choice wines, juicy, rich food and pure, choice wines" (Isa 25:6).

The eschatological banquet is a constant leitmotif in the life of Jesus. At the very beginning of His public ministry, Jesus heralds this messianic feast promised by Isaiah. At Cana, when the wine provided by the bride and bridegroom runs out, Jesus turns more than one hundred and twenty gallons of water into a choice wine of rare vintage. More wine than can be consumed by the already sated guests. A sign of the abundance of the last times.

During His ministry, Jesus feeds the five thousand men, not counting the women and children. The miracle is so unforgettable that all four evangelists record it (Mt 14:13-21; Mk 6:31-44; Lk 9:10-17 and Jn 6:5-15). The miracle begins with five loaves of barley bread and two dried fish, but it ends with twelve baskets overflowing with the leftovers. More food at the end than at the beginning. Again a foreshadowing of the final banquet when God will provide enough for us to feast on forever.

Throughout His ministry, Jesus often uses a banquet or meal either as an occasion to teach about the kingdom of God. In fact, at the Last Supper, when wine turns into blood, Jesus gives His Church the way to share even now in the eschatological banquet. He gives us the Eucharist where we are at table with Jesus in the Upper Room and already at God's banquet in heaven.

When Jesus' contemporaries witnessed His ministry, many thrilled to His teaching, marveled at His miracles, and stood in awe at His exorcisms. But, beyond the preaching, the healing, and the mighty works, there was one aspect of Jesus ministry that His enemies consistently found offensive. It was His table-fellowship with sinners. So often is Jesus either at a meal, going to a meal, or leaving a meal, that His enemies grumble, "He is a glutton and a drunkard, a friend of tax collectors and sinners" (Lk 7:34).

Jesus justifies His table-fellowship with sinners by announcing that "the Son of Man has come to seek out

The Parable of the Great Banquet

and to save what was lost" (Lk 19:10). It is quite significant that Jesus makes this remark in the course of a meal in the home of the notorious and hated tax collector Zacchaeus. It was in sharing meals with both the pious and the sinner that Jesus not only taught about the kingdom, but made the kingdom of God open to all, offering everyone a place at the final banquet.

Ten times in the gospel of Luke, Jesus is found at table with others. He dines with friends such as Martha and Mary (Lk 10:38-42) and with his own disciples (Lk 22:14-38; 24:28-35, 36-43). He shares a meal with the crowds who follow Him (Lk 9:10-17). He accepts the hospitality of the religious leaders and the elite (Lk 7:36; 11:37-52; 14:1-24). And Jesus is not afraid to sit at table with the outcasts and sinners (Lk 5:27-32; 19:1-10).

No other New Testament writer emphasizes the table-fellowship of Jesus more than Luke. In fact, "in approximately one-fifth of the sentences in Luke's Gospel and in Acts, meals play a conspicuous role" (Markus Barth, *Rediscovering the Lord's Supper*, p. 71). Why is this table-fellowship so important for Jesus?

In every culture, meals are a strong expression of friendship and acceptance. In Jesus' day, people were clearly divided by social position and religious practice. At meals, these boundaries were especially observed. People knew with whom they could eat. They knew where they were not welcome. Jesus demonstrated a total freedom from these restrictive conventions of His day. His choice of dinner companions was deliberately inclusive. He was offering God's grace to all.

In Luke's gospel, Jesus tells a parable whose theological truth ranks it next to the famous parable of the Prodigal Son. It is the parable of the Great Banquet. Everything Jesus says about divine mercy and human response is contained in this magnificent story. Everything Jesus taught by His own table-fellowship with others is brought to light in this memorable tale. And Jesus tells this parable in the context of a meal.

One day, a leader of the Pharisees invites Jesus for a Sabbath meal. Jesus graciously accepts the invitation. In the course of the dinner, He notices the guests jostling for seats of honor. He understands the secret motives of those present, including His host.

These were individuals who were accustomed to invite to their table only those who could add to their own prestige and then would repay them in kind. Their banquets were feasts of pride. Jesus first instructs them on humility and the disinterested charity necessary for the kingdom of God. Then, in response to a guest who exclaims, "Blessed is the man who will dine in the kingdom of God," (Lk 14:15), Jesus tells the parable of the Great Banquet.

> A man gave a sumptuous banquet, to which he invited many. When the hour for the banquet drew near, he sent his servant to say to those who had been invited: "Come, for everything is now ready."
>
> But one after another they all began to make excuses. The first said, "I have bought a parcel of land, and I must go out to inspect it. Please accept my apologies." Another said, "I have purchased five yoke of oxen, and I am on my way to try them out. Please accept my regrets." Still another said, "I have just gotten married, and therefore I am unable to come."
>
> When the servant returned, he reported all this to his master. Then the owner of the house became enraged, and he said to his servant, "Go out quickly into the streets and alleys of the town and bring in here the poor, the crippled, the blind, and the lame."

The Parable of the Great Banquet

Shortly afterward, the servant told him, "Sir, your orders have been carried out, and some room is still available." Then the master said to the servant, "Go out to the open roads and along the hedgerows and compel people to come, so that my house may be filled."   *Lk 14:16-23*

Jesus' use of the image of a feast conveys the joy of being His follower. It reminds us that a sober face is not the sign of a great holiness. In Matthew's gospel, this same parable is recorded (Mt 22:1-10). But there are many allegorical elements added. The banquet becomes a wedding feast. The man becomes a king. And, when enraged, he sends out a punitive expedition to destroy his enemies.

Luke's version of the parable is clear and straightforward. As Luke gives us the parable, Jesus' message is easily heard. God invites all to feast with Him in the kingdom of heaven. Those invited are free to accept or reject His gracious invitation.

Jesus' listeners were anxiously waiting for the moment when God would break into history to usher in the kingdom of God. They were expecting that, when He did, God would provide a great feast for His people. As Jesus tells this parable, they immediately think of that banquet and the arrival of the kingdom of God. They judge themselves as the only ones worthy to take part in this banquet. But Jesus challenges their narrow-mindedness with a glimpse at the mercy of God.

According to the custom of the time, a host would always send two invitations to his guests. The first invitation would simply announce the day of the great banquet. In order to prepare for the feast, the host had to know in advance the number of guests.

If there were only a few people, the host would serve chicken. If there were more than thirty-five guests, he would butcher a calf. In a time when people did not regulate their lives by the hours on a wrist watch, the second invitation would come on the day of the banquet, informing the guests that everything was ready.

In the parable, those invited accept the first invitation. At the minimum, the host slaughters one calf. This is going to be a lavish banquet. But, when the second invitation comes, the invited guests, one by one, excuse themselves. Their reasons for no longer coming are pathetic.

No one would buy a field without first having thoroughly examined it, determined its stone wall boundaries, and calculated its anticipated rainfall. No one would buy five yoke of oxen without first having plowed with them to see if they were fit for work. And certainly no bridegroom would ever have accepted the first invitation if his wedding was on the same day. They made their excuses not because they *could* not come, but because they *would* not come.

Jesus deliberately chooses these three excuses because they are so ludicrous. No one would seriously offer them to a man of prestige as is the host of this banquet. With a bit of humor, Jesus is lampooning the lame excuses that we so often place in the way of responding to God's invitation to feast at His table. God is ever ready to offer us His love and mercy. Yet we let work, possessions, emotions, and human affection keep us from entering into a deeper relationship with God. How foolish not to place God first!

Jesus carefully crafts the three excuses of the rude guests in the parable from His own store of biblical knowledge. In Deuteronomy 20:5-7 and 24:5, these same

The Parable of the Great Banquet

excuses were accepted as reasons not to take part in a holy war. His audience, learned in the Scriptures, gets His point. What was once a valid exemption is no more. Jesus is waging a campaign to establish the kingdom of God. The moment is urgent. No time to delay a response.

The gospels record Jesus crying twice. Both times at death. At the death of his friend Lazarus (Jn 11:35). And, at the death of good intentions when Jerusalem delays responding to His invitation to enter the kingdom and thus insures its own destruction (Lk 19:41). May we respond today!

After the original guests refuse to come to the banquet, the poor and the crippled, the blind and the lame are invited. When the banquet is not yet filled, the master then orders his servant to go out into the public highways and roads and compel those invited to come. The word "compel" (ἀνάγκασον: anankason) is highly significant.

In the very first place, it expresses the strong, undiminished desire of the master to have a full house. God's plan for the salvation of humankind is not to be hindered by man's sins. God is relentless in His love.

In the second place, the word shows God's understanding of human nature. Those invited feel unworthy. They recognize their own poverty and they feel hesitant to accept an invitation to such a noble banquet. Compelling them does not mean bringing them in by force. It means urging them, persuading them, convincing them that the master knows who they are and truly wants them at his table.

In a healthy self-examination of conscience, we may linger over our sins that keep us from responding to God's presence in our lives. In the parable that Jesus tells, He redirects our perspective. He emphasizes not our sins, but God's unrelenting offer of grace. As Isaiah the prophet said, God is ready to "sweep away your transgressions like a cloud, your sins like a mist" (Isa 44:22).

Jesus uses the details in the parable of the Great Banquet to show how much God desires all to accept His invitation. First, there is the double invitation to the original guests. After their refusal, two more invitations to others. Then there follows the bringing in of the substitute guests. Those from inside the town are the poor, the crippled, the blind, and the lame, the outcasts of Jewish society. Those from outside the town are the Gentiles. There is no road that God does not take to reach everyone. He even took the road to Calvary where the Cross flings open the door to the Messianic banquet.

Jesus' words in the parable "Come, for everything is now ready" are a prophecy of His final words on the Cross "It is finished." In His death, Jesus fulfills the eternal plan of God to open the way into the kingdom.

Jesus' death on the Cross was no common death. Our guilt condemned the innocent One. Our shameless deeds fashioned the wood of a tree into the Cross. Our sinful pleasure pierced Him through with unutterable pain. Nonetheless, knowing what was before Him, Jesus said, "No one takes [my life] from me. I lay it down of my own free will" (Jn 10:18).

Jesus goes to the Cross, because this is God's will to save the world. As Jesus explains to the Greeks in the last week of His life, "And when I am lifted up from the earth, I will draw all to myself" (Jn 12:32). Because of the Cross, God "casts aside . . . not one of His servants, loathes no one as unworthy of His divine mysteries . . . having mercy on all, and desiring to save all, wanting to make all sons of God..." (St. Hippolytus, *De Antichristo* 3). This is God's grace.

The Parable of the Great Banquet

This is not the "cheap grace we bestow on ourselves ...the preaching of forgiveness without requiring repentance, ...grace without discipleship, grace without the cross, grace without Jesus Christ, living and incarnate... [It is] costly grace... which must be sought again and again, the gift which must be asked for, the door at which a man must knock. Such grace is costly because it calls us to follow Jesus Christ. It is costly because it costs a man his life, and it is grace because it gives a man the only true life" (Dietrich Bonhoeffer, *The Cost of Discipleship*, pp. 43-47).

In Christ Crucified and Risen, present in the Eucharist, the Father sets before us the eschatological feast. Christ himself, the Lamb slain who dies no more, is the feast of truth for our questioning minds, the pardon for our sinful wills and the joy for all the yearnings and desires of our hearts.

Jesus is the bread that nourishes us during our earthly pilgrimage. The true manna come down from heaven. He is the wine that cheers our hearts and lifts up our souls. Thus, every Eucharist is the banquet that Isaiah predicted for the end time.

When we celebrate Mass, "we are united to the heavenly 'liturgy' and become part of that great multitude which cries out: 'Salvation belongs to our God, who sits on the throne and to the Lamb!' (Rev 7:10). The Eucharist is truly a glimpse of heaven appearing on earth. It is a glorious ray of the heavenly Jerusalem which pierces the clouds of our history and lights up our journey" (Pope St. John Paul, *Ecclesia de Eucharistia*, 19).

Today, there are some who do not respond to Jesus' invitation to be seated at His table. The preacher is boring. The music dull. The liturgy too long. The excuses may be different, but the refusal is the same. In every case, what is needed is not a new voice, a new song, a more exciting service. What is needed is a change of heart! A heart of gratitude open to God's grace.

Jesus began His parable of the Great Banquet with the imperative: "Come, everything is now ready." He ended the parable with the same urgent request, "Make people come in that my home may be filled." Our place is ready. The door is still open. And, God is waiting for us. It is all grace. It is all a free gift. It is our awesome responsibility to respond to His invitation today.

CHAPTER 13

The Parable of the Useless Servant

George Washington had such a great influence on the founding of the United States that he is known as the "Father of his country." Because he was a legend in his own day, many stories about him began to be circulated. There is the most famous, iconic story about his chopping down his father's cherry tree and then telling his father the truth. There is the folk legend of his throwing a silver dollar across the Potomac River. In these stories, fact and fiction join hands. But there is one particular historical story that reveals the true greatness of America's first president; and, it is fact.

On Saturday, March 15, 1783, some disgruntled officers were meeting in Newburgh, New York to discuss a military coup against Congress. Washington showed up unexpectedly. He had a letter in hand from a member of Congress. But he had great difficulty in reading it. The officers anxiously watched as he just stared at the letter, not saying a word.

Then, ever so cautiously, Washington pulled from his pocket something the officers had never seen him use. He put on a pair of eyeglasses that only his closest associates knew he wore. Finally, he spoke. "Gentlemen," he said, "you will permit me to put on my spectacles, for I have not only grown gray but almost blind in the service of my country." The rebel soldiers wept. They dropped their plans for a coup. Washington's humility did what his arguments could not do. It saved the country.

Washington was truly a humble man. He served as commander-in-chief of the colonial armies in the American Revolution. He successfully led an undisciplined army against the British Empire. He presided over the convention that produced the Constitution of the United States. Twice he was elected President of the United States. At the end of his long, dedicated service to his country, he was content to slip out of the spotlight, away from the acclaim. In returning to his private estate in Mount Vernon, he remarked to his colleagues, "Gentlemen, if you wish to speak to me again, it will be under my own fig tree and vine." He was truly humble.

True greatness is born of humility. "Do you wish to rise? Begin by descending. You plan a tower that will pierce the clouds? Lay first the foundation of humility" (Saint Augustine). This is true both in the world and in the kingdom of God. Humility is the soul of every virtue and the source of every noble deed. In the following parable of the Useless Servant, Jesus extols the importance of humility for His followers.

> Which of you, when your servant returns from plowing or tending sheep in the fields, would say to him, "Come right away and sit down to eat"? Would you not rather say, "Prepare my dinner, put on your apron, and wait on me while I eat and drink, and then afterward you yourself may eat and drink"? Would you be grateful to that servant for doing what he was commanded? So should it be with you. When you have done all that you were ordered to do, say, "We are unprofitable servants; we have only done our duty." *Lk 17:7-10*

Only Luke records this parable which Jesus addresses to His disciples. The evangelist gives no indication of the context. We do not know when or where Jesus spoke this parable. Nonetheless, this parable certainly fits the general context of Jesus' ministry.

Like other pious Jews, the disciples of Jesus held that God rewards those who are faithful to the covenant and punishes those who are not. They believed that they would receive blessings in this world (Deut 18:1-14) and a reward in the world to come (Dan 12:3). Divine retribution goes hand and hand with divine justice. As the psalmist says, "The just shall rejoice to see the vengeance and bathe their feet in the blood of the wicked. Then people will say: 'Truly there is a reward for the righteous; there is a God who dispenses justice on the earth'" (Ps 58:12).

All three synoptic gospels remember the day when Peter questioned Jesus about the rewards that the disciples would receive for following Him. Characteristically unafraid to speak up, Peter voices what the others were surely thinking. "We have given up everything and followed you. What will there be for us?" (Mt 19:27; Mk 10:28; Lk 18:28). It was perfectly natural for Peter to ask Jesus this question.

When Jesus sent the seventy-two disciples on mission, He Himself said that "the laborer deserves his wages" (Lk 10:7). So asking Jesus what special reward the disciples would receive for serving Him with their lives was not an inappropriate question. With the parable of the Useless Servant, Jesus provides an answer.

In the parable, Jesus speaks of a servant. The Greek word is δοῦλος (doulos). This is not an employee hired to work for a certain number of hours, but a servant or slave under the complete authority of his master. Some servants or slaves were purchased with money. Others were taken as captive in war. In either case, they were wholly at the disposition of their owner.

Servants were legally bound to do whatever the master commanded. They would care for the crops, planting them and harvesting them. They would pasture the goats and sheep, feeding and protecting them. They would do the needed domestic chores. Never would the servant expect the owner to thank him for doing what duty demanded.

Jesus uses the example of such a servant coming in after a hard day's work in the fields. Tired and worn out, he prepares supper for the owner and does not look to be thanked. The master eats first. Only then does the servant have his meal. The master's needs take precedence over his.

Jesus ends the parable with a question to His disciples. The disciples are at times slow to understand (Mk 4:10-13; 6:52; 8:7-18). So Jesus frames His question so as to provoke the correct answer. "The master does not thank the servant for doing what he was commanded to do, does he?"

As they shake their heads, giving "no" as the answer, Jesus continues. "So should it be with you. When you have done all you have been commanded, say, 'We are unprofitable servants; we have done what we were obliged to do.'" Jesus makes sure they do not miss the point of His parable.

The expression "unprofitable servant" or "useless servant" (δοῦλος ἀχρεῖος: doulos archeios) seems a strange name for someone who has worked so hard for his master. However, it simply means that the servant who does what is his duty has no claim on his master. He has done no favor for which he can demand compensation.

In a certain sense, the parable of the Useless Servant is the least attractive of all the parables Jesus told. It represents God under an image so contrary to the normal way Jesus speaks about God. We find comfort when He speaks about God as a caring shepherd looking after his flock or as an anxious woman in search of a lost coin or as a wealthy man throwing open the doors of his banquet to the poor and marginalized. These are images of mercy and compassion. How can we even begin to reconcile these consoling images of God with that of an insensitive owner, a hard, ungrateful taskmaster as portrayed in the parable?

We must take into account that Jesus uses the protagonists in His parables sometimes to make a comparison with God and at other times to show a contrast. He paints the uncomplimentary picture of an unjust judge (Lk 18: 1-8) and the man who is awakened by a friend during the night (Lk 11:5-13). These characters do what is good for others only because they are forced to do so. But God is not like that! He needs neither to be cajoled nor to be prodded. He is eager to do what helps us.

In the parable of the Prodigal Son, the younger and the elder brother both see their relationship to their father in terms of servile obedience. But the father does not look at them as his servants. They are both his beloved sons. He forgives the prodigal son. He holds open the door to feasting and rejoicing for his older son.

We are God's beloved sons and daughters; and, He wants us to call him "Abba" (Daddy). When we go to God with our needs, we are knocking on an open door. As Jesus says, "If you then, despite your evil nature, know how to give good gifts to your children, how much more will your heavenly Father give good things to those who ask him" (Mt 7:11).

The more we are aware of all that God gives us, the less we will complain about our obedience to Him and the more patient we will be when He expects more of us. "It is not hard to obey when we love the one whom we obey" (St. Ignatius). So important is obedience that Jesus Himself said, "I came down from heaven not to do my own will but the will of him who sent me" (Jn 6:38). Obedience to God is the freedom to love.

Many today cringe at the very word "obedience." They echo the words which Mozart put on the lips of Don Giovanni's servant: *Non voglio più servir* (I will serve no more). Technology and science have deceived some into thinking that we are masters responsible to no one. Supreme Court Justice Anthony Kennedy canonized this view when he said, "At the heart of liberty is the right to define one's own concept of existence, of meaning, of the universe and of the mystery of human life" (*Planned Parenthood v. Casey*, 1992).

Kennedy's opinion gave voice to the unbridled relativism of our post-Christian age. It is the perfect recipe for chaos. It promotes a worldview without God. Man himself sits proudly on the throne of judgment.

The parable of the Useless Servant goes against this pride of modern society. The parable makes clear the stark reality of human existence. God is God and we are not! "We have come to see ourselves as…lords and masters, entitled to plunder [the earth] at will" (Pope Francis, *Laudato Si*, 2). For the world and for us to flourish, we need humility to recognize that we are creatures and God alone is Creator and Lord. It is His will that we must do.

> We are God's servants; we are not his creditors but we are always debtors in relation to him because we owe him everything, because everything is his gift. Accepting and doing his will is the way that we must live every day, in every moment of

our life. Before God we must not present ourselves as those who believe that they have done a service and deserve a great recompense.
Pope Benedict XVI, Homily, October 3, 2010

Everything we have, we receive from God. They are His gifts on loan to us for the common good. "The rich man who gives to the poor does not bestow alms but pays a debt" (St. Ambrose). Not only our ability to do good, but the very will to do good is a gift from God (Phil 2:13). Thus, "when God crowns our merits, he is only crowning his own gifts" (St. Augustine).

True humility makes us acknowledge the reality of our total dependence on God. It opens our eyes to our place in His plan. Humility is not weakness. It is the doorway to true greatness. In fact, only when we take the lowly attitude of a child, we become great in the kingdom of our heavenly Father (Mt 18:3-4). Humility is the glad trust in God who strengthens us in all we do (Phil 4:13).

Serving God in obedience at all times is indeed an arduous task. In the fourth century, the British monk Pelagius taught that we have the ability on our own to obey God and to earn our place in heaven. Pelagius was the lineal descendant of the Pharisees who taught obedience leads to God. But it is otherwise. God leads us to obedience. St. Augustine refuted Pelagius' misguided teaching. He taught that it is only by God's grace that we can we obey God and do good. We cannot earn our way into heaven.

We have no absolute claim on a reward from God. We are children of Adam and Eve. Our human nature is weak and sinful. The good we do, we do by the grace of God, not by the strength of our will. However, God does not ignore our efforts. He sees our desire to do what He asks of us. He acknowledges the good we do when we obey Him and is generous in His response.

St. Josemaria Escriva, founder of Opus Dei, once offered a telling example of God's response to our obedience. He said, "The lake of Gennesareth had denied its fishes to Peter's nets. A whole night in vain. Then, obedient, he lowered his net again to the water and they caught 'a huge number of fish.' Believe me: the miracle is repeated each day."

The greatest reward of obedience, however, is not the gifts God gives us. Rather, it is God who gifts us with Himself. "Whoever loves me will keep my word, and my Father will love him, and we will come to him and make our abode with him" (Jn 14:23). Truly, He does not see us as useless servants!

CONCLUSION

The 6th century Greek philosopher Heraclitus of Ephesus compared life to a river that is always flowing and never stays the same. He said that we can never step into the same river twice. Once we take our foot out of the water, that water is gone and is replaced with water from upstream. Key to Heraclitus' philosophy was this idea of constant change. He summed it up in the axiom Πάντα ῥεῖ (panta rhei) i.e., everything flows. Even a superficial look at history seems to prove him right.

Governments rise and fail. Science discards old theories. New technologies appear. Social values change. Freedom is constantly being tested. At times, some laws guarantee basic human rights. At other times, laws construct rights contrary to the law of God. One generation blesses what the previous disdained.

Individuals are constantly facing change. The industrious become affluent. The rich become poor. The healthy lose their strength. The caregiver needs to be cared for. How often the pleasures of this world turn into the bitter cup of suffering and the fresh vigor of youth fades into feeble old age!

In the midst of a sea of change, with the billows swirling about us, there remains one sure rock that steadies our course. That rock is Christ. The sun rises and sets. Years slip into centuries, but Christ remains the same. "Jesus Christ is the same yesterday and today and forever" (Heb 13:8).

Some individuals strut across the stage of history, capturing the applause of the masses. But, when the curtain comes down, someone else takes their place in the drama of life. But no one can ever take the place of Jesus. He is "the true light which enlightens everyone coming into the world" (Jn 1:9). His teachings do not gather dust. They do not remain on the printed text of some scholarly tome. They take on flesh in the life of His followers. His teachings are the bread of life for those hungering for the truth.

Civilizations have come and gone. Yet, every age continues to find new meaning and fresh strength in the parables Jesus told. He related these stories along the shores of the Sea of Galilee, in the houses of His disciples, at dinner parties with the elite and the marginalized, and in the courtyard of the Jerusalem Temple. But these narratives are not tied to one place and one time.

As narratives, the parables are art and thus have the potential to receive new and deeper interpretations. As stories coming from the lips of the Word made flesh, these parables challenge the listener in every generation. We may interpret the parables, but, as the inspired word of God, they ultimately interpret us.

> Indeed, the word of God is living and active. Sharper than any two-edged sword, it pierces to the point where it divides soul and spirit, joints and marrow; it judges the thoughts and the intentions of the heart. Nothing in creation is hidden from his sight. Everything is uncovered and exposed to the eyes of the one to whom we must all render an account.
> *Heb 4:12-13*

The parables open us up to the heart of Jesus. On the Cross, His pierced heart revealed the depth of God's love. The parables expose in literary form that same love beckoning all to enter the kingdom of heaven. To return again and again to the parables is to come closer and closer to the very heart of God. These are not stories to be read and then tossed aside, but invitations to enter into a deeper union with God who is love.

Much of today's preaching is moralistic. It aims at putting us on the narrow path that leads to heaven. But the parables, with the use of metaphor, function in a different manner. They are images to open wide the door of God's grace in the very moment we listen to them.

The parables bring us face to face with the mystery of God who "makes his sun rise on the bad and the good, and causes rain to fall on the righteous and the wicked" (Mt 5:45). They overturn our standards of human conduct. They make us feel beneath our feet the tremors of a new world in its birthing. When we meditate on the words of Jesus, we find delight and become "like a tree planted near streams of water, which bears its fruit in season and whose leaves never wither" (Ps 1:2-3).

The memorable images of Jesus' parables remain embedded in our minds. The Good Samaritan. The father of the prodigal son. The tax collector beating his breast. The farmer looking for figs. The seed planted in the ground. The tower collapsing. The rich man clothed in purple and feasting with Lazarus in rags begging at his doorstep. The parables shine the divine light on the experiences of this world and, through them, lead us to God.

The parables make us realize that God does not only occasionally intervene in our lives, but rather is always present. These narratives crack the shell of mundane reality to expose the divine in the human, the supernatural in the worldly. They strike the rock of everyday life to let flow "rivers of living water" (Jn 7:38).

The parables challenge. They excite. They inspire. They confront our freedom and offer us the choice of accepting God's transforming grace in the present moment of our lives. They are the invitation to enter the kingdom of God which, like the seed sown in good ground, is slowly maturing to completion.

The world may delude itself into thinking it is done with Christ. But Christ is not done with the world. He is no less present to this generation than He was to His first century listeners. Jesus says to each of us who listen to His parables, "Heaven and earth will pass away, but my words will never pass away" (Mt 24:35).

Through the appeal of His parables and the grace they offer, Jesus is building up the kingdom of God. Those who do not believe in God are attempting to build a lasting city that will crumble and fall. But those who build upon the rock foundation of Jesus, the Eternal Word, can face the raging storms and winds of this world and remain secure unto eternity.

JESUS' LAST DAYS

Most Rev. Arthur J. Serratelli, S.T.D., S.S.L., D.D.

The Cross was part of God's plan to bring Jesus to glory; and, it remains the instrument of our salvation. The Cross still speaks to the believer. For this reason, I offer the following biblical meditations on specific moments of the Passion narrative. In our own life, we are called to walk with Jesus in joy and in suffering. His Cross continues to enable us in every event of our life to discover God.

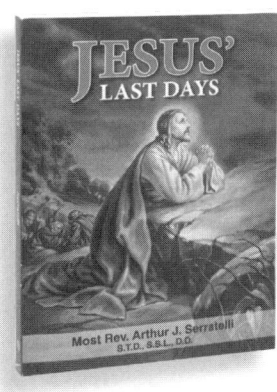

A deeper understanding of the events of Jesus' last days as recorded in Scripture can help us to see more clearly our own call to discipleship today.

—*From the Author's Introduction*

Through Bishop Serratelli's reflections on the similar accounts of the four evangelists, we relive Jesus' Passion bathed in the light of Easter glory. We will appreciate how the Cross remains the instrument of our salvation and see more clearly our own call to discipleship. 128 pages. Size 5 x 7.

No. 932/04—Flexible cover **6.95**
ISBN 978-1-9-47070-35-6

catholicbookpublishing.com

THE SEVEN GIFTS OF THE HOLY SPIRIT

Most Rev. Arthur J. Serratelli, S.T.D., S.S.L., D.D.

Jesus alone possessed the seven gifts of the Holy Spirit in their fullness. But, the Holy Spirit graciously gives those same gifts to all who follow Jesus.

The seven gifts are our inheritance as baptized and confirmed Christians. We do not earn them. We do not merit them. They are given to us gratuitously. They make us open to the promptings of the Holy Spirit in our lives. They help us grow in holiness, making us fit for heaven. These seven gifts of the Holy Spirit help us live a truly authentic Christian way of life.

—From the Author's Introduction

Through history, art, Scripture, and Catholic documents, you will appreciate and grasp more fully how the seven gifts of the Holy Spirit can help you to live a truly authentic Christian life filled with peace and joy. 96 pages. Size $4^{3}/_{8}$ x $6^{3}/_{4}$.

No. 930/04—Flexible cover **5.95**
ISBN 978-1-947070-23-3

catholicbookpublishing.com

FROM THE CROSS TO THE EMPTY TOMB

Most Rev. Arthur J. Serratelli, S.T.D., S.S.L., D.D.

As Christians, we make our life-journey in union with Christ Crucified. The *Via Crucis* is the school of Christian life. As Peter once asked Jesus, the world questions each of us today, *"Quo Vadis?"* "Where are you going?" It will help each of us respond to this question by accompanying Jesus on the Way to the Cross. I offer the following brief meditations on individuals who were with Jesus in the last hours of His own life on earth.

—From the Author's Introduction

The author invites you to journey with those who were with Jesus in His last hours. You may be like Peter one day, and like Judas, Simon, Mary Magdalene, or Our Lady on another. This Lenten book provides a deeper appreciation for God's eternal saving love. 96 pages. Size 4 3/8 x 6 3/4.

No. 928/04—Flexible cover **6.95**
ISBN 978-1-947070-13-4

catholicbookpublishing.com

St. Joseph BIBLE HANDBOOK — In addition to a general introduction to each book of the Bible, the main headings found in every book—the *Outline, Frequently Asked Questions, Study Questions,* and *Look out for…*— succinctly point to the valuable information contained in the pages of the Bible. 256 pages. Size 6¾ x 9½.

No. 649/04—Durable cover **19.95**
ISBN 978-1-941243-98-5

St. Joseph NEW CATHOLIC BIBLE NEW TESTAMENT — This readable study edition has a large, easy-to-read typeface, complete notes and references, self-explaining maps, a handy Study Guide, a Bible Dictionary, the words of Christ in red, photographs, and many other features. Ideal for schools and Bible study. 528 pages. Size 6½ x 9¼.

No. 311/19—Burgundy Dura-Lux cover **17.95**
ISBN: 978-1-947070-66-0

LIVING WITH HOPE — By Cardinal Carlo Maria Martini, S.J. Reflecting on the author's pastoral thoughts on the actions and teachings of Jesus and the Church will help us to live in Christian hope and proclaim this hope to others. 192 pages. Size 5¼ x 7¾.

No. 167/04—Flexible cover............................**9.95**
ISBN 978-1-937913-78-6

DAILY MEDITATIONS WITH THE HOLY SPIRIT — By Rev. Jude Winkler, OFM Conv. Through daily Scripture readings and prayer, Fr. Winkler offers us an opportunity to develop a closer relationship with the Holy Spirit and to apply the fruits of our meditation to our everyday lives. 192 pages. Size 4 x 6¼.

No. 198/19—Dura-Lux cover **9.95**
ISBN 978-1-937913-56-4

catholicbookpublishing.com

St. Joseph FAMILY EDITION HOLY BIBLE — This Saint Joseph Family Edition is a distinguished addition to the NEW CATHOLIC BIBLE (NCB) offerings. The translation of the complete Old and New Testaments is fresh, faithful, and reader friendly. This edition boasts a distinctive, easy-to-read, and inviting 13-pt. typeface, the largest of any Catholic Family Bible in a comparable size. Its rich, extensive, and insightful footnotes are in a highly readable font. 1792 pages. Size 8 1/2 x 11.

No. 619/97—Simulated leather **59.00**
ISBN 978-1-9-47070-98-1

THE LITANY OF THE SACRED HEART — By Mario Collantes. This collection of 33 invocations with accompanying commentaries offers a meaningful way to express and nurture our love for the Person of Jesus, Who is the Source of our salvation and hope. Full color. 96 pages. Size 4 3/8 x 6 3/4.

No. 374/04—Flexible cover...............................**6.95**
ISBN 978-0-89942-366-1

JOYFULLY LIVING THE GOSPEL DAY BY DAY — By Rev. John Catoir. Each day contains a specific Scripture quotation, reflection, and prayer to encourage joyous participation in the Christian life. 192 pages. Size 4 x 6 1/4.

No. 188/19—Dura-Lux cover **9.95**
ISBN 978-1-937913-04-5

THE IMITATION OF CHRIST — by Thomas à Kempis. Prayer book size edition. This treasured book has brought peace to readers for many ages by showing how to follow the life of Christ to which all are called. Includes a full-color Rosary and Stations of the Cross section. 288 pages. Size 4 x 6 1/4.

No. 320/19—Dura-Lux cover **12.95**
ISBN 978-1-941243-16-9

catholicbookpublishing.com

Bishop Emeritus Arthur J. Serratelli was the seventh bishop of the Diocese of Paterson, N.J. He is present chairman for the Vatican's Dialogue between the Catholic Church and the World Alliance of Baptists. He has served as chairman of the International Commission on English in the Liturgy; member of the Vatican's Congregation of Divine Worship and the Discipline of the Sacraments; and member of Vox Clara. He has served a three-year term as chairman of the Committee for the Translation of Sacred Scripture of the United States Conference of Catholic Bishops; twice chairman of the Committee on Divine Worship of the United States Conference of Catholic Bishops; chairman of the Committee on Doctrine; and member of the Subcommittee for the Review of Catechetical Texts. As a Professor of Sacred Scripture and Systematics, he has taught in three major seminaries. He continues to give retreats, lectures, and courses in Sacred Scripture as well as doing pastoral work in a parish.

    This is the Bishop's fourth book. His previous books are: *From the Cross to the Empty Tomb*, *The Seven Gifts of the Holy Spirit*, and *Jesus' Last Days*.